LECTURES

ON THE

GROWTH OF CRIMINAL LAW

IN

ANCIENT COMMUNITIES

BY

RICHARD R. CHERRY, LL.D.
BARRISTER-AT-LAW;
REID PROFESSOR OF CONSTITUTIONAL AND CRIMINAL LAW IN THE
UNIVERSITY OF DUBLIN

Οὗτοι νόμον μὴ ἔχοντες,
ἑαυτοῖς εἰσι νόμος

THE LAWBOOK EXCHANGE, LTD.
Union, New Jersey
2001

ISBN 1-58477-167-4

Third printing 2004

Printed in the United States of America on acid-free paper

THE LAWBOOK EXCHANGE, LTD.
33 Terminal Avenue
Clark, New Jersey 07066-1321

Please see our website for a selection of our other publications and fine facsimile reprints of classic works of legal history:
www.lawbookexchange.com

Library of Congress Cataloging-in-Publication Data

Cherry, Richard R. (Richard Robert), 1859-1923
Lectures on the growth of criminal law in ancient communities / by Richard R. Cherry.
p. cm.
Originally published: London: Macmillan and Co., 1890.
Includes bibliographical references and index.
ISBN 1-58477-167-4 (cloth: alk. paper)
1. Criminal law--History. 2. Law, Ancient. I. Title.

K5032 .C49 2001
345'.009--dc21

00-067010

LECTURES

ON THE

GROWTH OF CRIMINAL LAW

IN

ANCIENT COMMUNITIES

BY

RICHARD R. CHERRY, LL.D.

BARRISTER-AT-LAW;

REID PROFESSOR OF CONSTITUTIONAL AND CRIMINAL LAW IN THE
UNIVERSITY OF DUBLIN

Οὗτοι νόμον μὴ ἔχοντες,
ἑαυτοῖς εἰσι νόμος

London
MACMILLAN AND CO.
AND NEW YORK
1890

DUBLIN:
PRINTED AT THE UNIVERSITY PRESS,
BY PONSONBY AND WELDRICK.

PREFACE.

IN the six lectures contained in the present volume I have attempted, as briefly as possible, to compare the early ideas of several nations as to crimes and their punishment. I have selected legal systems as far apart from, and as much independent of, each other as possible, with a view to showing that identity of usage did not arise from the adoption by one nation of the laws or institutions of another, but rather from the inherent principles of human nature. The close similarity between the early institutions of very distant races as regards Penal Law is extremely remarkable. Nothing illustrates so much the complete contrast between modern and ancient ideas, on legal subjects, as the study of this branch of Law historically. The existence of Law, without any Sovereign authority—without any sanction, or recognized tribunal—seems to us almost a contradiction in terms. Yet, it was out of such a state of society that Law developed itself in all its branches, gradually and slowly. In the study of Criminal Law, we really have a test of the validity of the historical method. We can easily understand how such matters as the laws of inheritance and contract arose from custom, for even to the present day we recognize, in some degree, the binding force of customs in these branches of Law; but it is difficult to believe that Criminal Law could have originated in the same manner. Criminal Law naturally seems, even in its earliest stage, to be a restriction upon custom—a system of commands, necessarily, we would suppose, imposed by some political superior, to restrain the practice of customs which were disapproved of, rather than to sanction those already observed.

It appears to have been from the Criminal Law that the Analytical School of Jurisprudence derived its very notion of Law. To show, therefore, that the origin of Criminal, as well as of other branches of Law, was in primeval custom, is extremely important. My object, in these lectures, has been to do so, and at the same time to point out the traces of primitive ideas which remain in later developments of Criminal Law. I am aware that I have only carried out this object in a very imperfect and "sketchy" manner, but I could do no more than this in the limited number of lectures which a Professor of Law may legitimately devote to such an abstract subject.

The substance of the second lecture on Ancient Irish Law is taken from an article which I wrote some time ago in the *Law Magazine and Review*. It was the study of the Brehon Laws which completely satisfied Sir Henry Maine as to the validity of his historical method as applied to Civil Law. I do not think anyone who reads the *Book of Aicill*, however cursorily, can doubt that his method applies equally well to Criminal or Penal Law. The same state of affairs, as the *Book of Aicill* exhibits to us as existing in ancient Ireland, seems to have prevailed in all other nations at one period of their progress, though only traces of its existence remain elsewhere in the maturer laws of a more settled state of society.

R. R. CHERRY.

TRINITY COLLEGE, DUBLIN,
October, 1890.

CONTENTS.

LECTURE I.

INTRODUCTORY.

PRIMITIVE CUSTOM AS TO CRIMES.

LECTURE II.

ANCIENT IRISH LAW.

LECTURE III.

LAW OF SEMITIC RACES.

I. HEBREW LAW.

II. MOHAMMEDAN LAW.

LECTURE IV.

ROMAN PENAL LAW.

LECTURE V.

EARLY ENGLISH PENAL LAW.

LECTURE VI.

EARLY ENGLISH CRIMINAL LAW.

LECTURE I.

INTRODUCTORY.

PRIMITIVE CUSTOM AS TO CRIMES.

My object, in the present Course of Lectures, is to trace historically the manner in which Criminal or Penal Law developed itself among ancient societies. The terms *Criminal Law* and *Penal Law* are by no means identical. Though with our modern notions we are apt to regard them as so, in the investigation of the laws of early communities the distinction between them must be clearly attended to. Penal Law is a term of wider signification than Criminal Law; it means that branch of law which deals with *punishment*, by whomsoever imposed and with whatsoever object. All Criminal Law is Penal in its nature, *i. e.* it effects its ends by means of punishment, but all Penal Law is not Criminal. There are still existing in our own legal system many penal actions of a civil nature, such as what are called *qui tam* actions, where a private individual seeks to recover a penalty for the violation of some statutory duty by another; but such actions have become so rare and unimportant that it has become usual with us to understand the terms "penal" and "criminal" as identical. In other systems of law, however, and especially in ancient legal systems, the principle of punishment is the foundation of a considerable portion of law which cannot be called criminal. Even in modern English law a great part of the law of torts is penal in its nature; and great confusion has been caused by the non-recognition of this fact in the rules which have been laid down at various times as to the measure of damages.

Criminal Law, as distinct from Penal Law, is difficult to define. A good description of the subject-matter to which the term is commonly applied will be found in Mr. Justice Stephen's *History of Criminal Law* (vol. I., pp. 2–4). As distinct from Penal Law, Criminal Law involves, I think, three elements: *firstly*, that the proceeding is of a public nature, instituted, in theory at least, by the State, or by some public authority representing the State, and not by the individual injured, in case any one individual is so injured; *secondly*, that the act upon which the proceedings are grounded, is, or is considered to be, a wrong or injury to society in general, and not to one person only. This is the characteristic most generally referred to as the distinguishing feature of Criminal Law; and, *thirdly*, as a logical consequence of the two former, that the offence cannot be purged by a subsequent compliance with the law violated, or by arrangement with the person primarily injured; the object of the punishment being, not to assist such person, but to protect society, by deterring others from committing similar offences. The public nature of the wrong which is punished, the public nature of the proceeding by which it is punished, and the public nature of the reasons for punishment will be found, on examination, to be present in every case which is considered in our law to be criminal in its character. The matter is of great practical importance to the lawyer, as upon the question, whether a proceeding is or is not of a criminal nature, depends the important question, whether an appeal lies under the Judicature Act from the decision of a Court of first instance or not. Imprisonment for contempt of Court is distinctly a proceeding of a punitive nature; still it is generally held to be a civil and not a criminal proceeding, for the object of the imprisonment is not so much to punish as to compel compliance with the law: and a person who has been committed for contempt can generally procure his release by doing the act for the refusal to do which the imprisonment was imposed. Thus, in a recent case where a witness was committed for refusing to answer a question in a bankruptcy matter under the 385th Section of the Bankruptcy (Ireland) Act, 1857, it was held by the Court of Appeal, upon this ground, that the proceeding was of a civil and not a criminal nature (*In re Keller*, 22 L. R. Ir., 158). "The refusal of a witness to answer a question may be a punishable contempt," says FitzGibbon, L. J., "but a proceeding taken, not to punish him, but to compel him to give evidence is not an exercise of punitive jurisdiction" (22 L. R. Ir., at p. 200). Similarly, imprisonment for debt under the old law was never considered to be criminal in its nature.

This distinction, as I have said, between Criminal and Penal Law is of the greatest importance in the study of primitive jurisprudence. It is pointed out by Sir H. Maine, in the 10th chapter of *Ancient Law*, that in early times the most important branch of the Law was Penal Law; but that, at the same time, true Criminal Law was almost entirely unknown.(*a*) The notion of an offence against the State is of entirely modern growth; and the theory that punishment is imposed for the sake of reforming the criminal and deterring others from following his example is even still more modern. It is extremely interesting to trace, historically, the growth of these ideas, and to show how Penal Law, and afterwards Criminal Law, gradually developed itself in different legal systems.

It is scarcely necessary, at the present day, to put forward any defence for the historical treatment of a legal subject. Still, I fear, the advantages of the historical method are more recognized in theory than appreciated in practice. Practical lawyers naturally confine their attention almost altogether to the law as it is, and disregard, or treat with contempt, historical disquisitions upon its origin; and this naturally leads students, who desire only to be practical lawyers, to follow their example.

(*a*) *Ancient Law*, pp. 369-371.

The analytical method of study, as it is called, has many grave defects, and one who pursues it alone will seldom or never become a really sound lawyer: for law is an art rather than a science, and a lawyer needs much more a knowledge of how to apply his principles than a mere verbal acquaintance with these principles themselves. The study of law in ordinary text-books, without an acquaintance with its history, is apt to encourage in the student one of the greatest faults in practice, namely, rash generalization. A student who pursues the method of Austin and Bentham alone is apt to suppose that law is like mathematics, certain and definite, and that its principles are applied, like the axioms of Euclid, with rigour and strictness to each case without variation. Every trained lawyer knows what immense difficulty there is in *applying* legal principles, and what caution and care are necessary in ascertaining the *ratio decidendi* of one case, and in applying it to another. A knowledge of the history of the branch of law with which any principle is connected is indeed absolutely necessary before its true bearings and the limits of its application can be fully understood. Principles are frequently applied quite illogically to different cases; and sometimes, in the course of the development of law, the true principle is forgotten, and an entirely wrong principle is invented to explain rules of law which are well established. The result is that the law is regulated, partly in accordance with one, and partly in accordance with another principle, and the application of each leads to entirely different results. In dealing with cases such as these, the abstract method of the analytical school of jurisprudence breaks down completely. A knowledge of the history of the law is necessary before one can at all understand the course of its development. Take, for instance, the well-established principle of the liability of a master for the wrongful acts of his servant when engaged in doing his master's business. We are all familiar with the rule that if a grocer's cart is driven carelessly by its driver, and in consequence of the driver's negligence any person is injured, the grocer is liable to an action. Here it is said that the principle of the master's liability is his negligence in employing an unskilful servant. If this were really so, the logical result would be, that if the master were guilty of no negligence in employing the servant, he would not be liable, or in other words, that a traverse of the master's personal negligence would be a good defence to the action. This is, however, not the case. It is no defence that the master used the greatest care in employing his servants. The real fact here is, that the theory of negligence is an after-thought, invented when the true principle of the action had been forgotten. The liability of the master is in reality a survival of the principle of the liability of an owner for the act of his *slave*, and is based on the same principle as his liability for injuries committed by animals in his possession. The historical investigation of the matter proves to us that the real basis of this liability is not any theory of negligence on the part of the master, but an entirely different one. In the Roman Law a class of actions existed called noxal actions, which provided for this case of vicarious liability. The defendant had the option of surrendering the delinquent instead of paying the damage. This right of avoiding liability by a surrender of the slave or animal has much puzzled lawyers, and the conjecture is probably true that the real origin of this feature of noxal actions was the right of private vengeance, which was recognized extensively in all bodies of ancient law. The origin of the liability appears to have been this—If an injury were done by a slave, the person injured had the right to exact vengeance against the slave personally, thus injuring the master's property; and the master or owner was consequently allowed to prevent this vengeance by making compensation for the injury done. The origin of the liability had, if this theory be true, nothing whatever to do with negligence on the part of the master, and, consequently, absence of negligence on his part was no defence to the action.

The noxal actions occupied a prominent position in Roman jurisprudence, but the later Roman jurists were as ignorant of their true origin as English lawyers formerly were, and dealt with the right of surrender (*noxæ deditio*) as if it were a limitation of liability, instead of being the original basis of the action (*a*). The duty of surrendering the criminal was the earliest obligation. As a substitute for this the master was allowed to pay damages.

There is very little doubt that the origin of the master's liability in our own law was exactly the same. The same right of surrender is mentioned in some of the older authorities as an alternative to liability in the case of injuries done by animals. In Fitzherbert's "Abridgment" it is stated to be law, that if a dog kill sheep, the owner of the dog can free himself from liability by giving up the dog to the owner of the sheep. This exactly corresponds with the *noxæ deditio* of the Roman Law; and when we go back still further, we find the duty of surrender stated to be the primary liability. By the laws of Ina, it is provided that "if a Wessex man slay an Englishman, then shall he who owns him deliver him up to the lord of the kindred, *or give* 60 *shillings for his life.*" How the principle came to be extended to the case of a hired servant it is difficult now to ascertain, but in all probability the origin of the liability was forgotten before slavery ceased to exist. This was undoubtedly so in the Roman Law.

The main defect of the analytical method is not, however, in the application of principles. It lies deeper, in that this method completely misinterprets the facts of ancient law. A law, according to the theory of Austin, consists of a command by a political superior to his subjects, the obedience to which is enforced by a punishment or penalty. As a matter of historical fact, however, ancient laws were not commands. They were not issued by political superiors, nor were they enforced by punishment or otherwise. They were merely customs, sanctioned by usage, voluntarily observed, with that strong devotion to usage which always characterizes uncivilized nations. "It is

(*a*) See on this question, Holmes's *Common Law*, p. 9. Moyle, *Inst. Just.*, 4, 8, 1 (note).

not," as Mr. Justice Stephen truly remarks, "till a very late stage of its history that law is regarded as a series of commands issued by the sovereign power of the State."(*a*) Law originated before any sovereign authority existed; and in England, at least, the king, even when he came to be recognized as in reality the sovereign authority, was in no sense superior to the law.

It is a matter of very great interest to ascertain, historically, the origin of Penal Law, and to trace the growth of ideas of crime in different legal systems. In order to do so, we must carefully note the points of agreement and difference between various systems, according to the differing political circumstances of each nation. The pursuit of the historical method always requires extreme caution. In the study of law, historically, there are, as Mr. O. W. Holmes says, two errors equally to be avoided: "one is that of supposing, because an idea seems very familiar and natural to us, that it has always been so. Many things which we take for granted have had to be laboriously fought out or thought out in past times. The other mistake is the opposite one of asking too much of history. We start with man fully grown. It may be assumed that the earliest barbarian, whose practices are to be considered, had a good many of the same feelings and passions as ourselves." (*b*)

If we select, for purposes of comparison, systems of law as widely apart from each other as possible; and if we find the same principle or the same practice prevailing in different communities, far removed from each other geographically, and unconnected with each other ethnologically, we may safely conclude that the common principle is one which takes its origin in human nature itself. The systems of Penal Law with which I propose to deal at present are the Brehon Laws of Ancient Ireland, the Hebrew Laws as exhibited to us in the Old Testament, the Mohammedan Law, the Roman Law, and

(*a*) *Digest of Criminal Law*, Introduction, p. xi. (*b*) *Common Law*, p. 2.

the Anglo-Saxon and Early English Laws. These different systems, representing, as they do, the different branches of the Aryan race, and also the two most important of the Semitic, exhibit, as a matter of fact, upon investigation, a striking similarity in the manner in which the rules upon the subject of crimes and punishments developed themselves in each.

The earliest view which we obtain of political society shows us in each case the same system prevailing for the redress of wrongs and punishment of offences, namely, a system of private revenge and personal redress of injuries. Each person avenged, in whatever manner he thought right, a wrong done him by another, and the customs of the tribe sanctioned his doing so with impunity. The idea of retaliation is one deeply rooted in man's nature. A savage or a child naturally revenges an injury by inflicting a similar one on the aggressor. Retribution in kind is viewed, even in civilized societies, with satisfaction. An eye for an eye, a tooth for a tooth; whoso sheddeth man's blood, by man shall his blood be shed—such is the rule in all early societies. As Mr. Moyle, in speaking of the Roman Law, well says: "A system of self-redress, in the form of private vengeance, preceded everywhere the establishment of a regular judicature; the injured person, with his kinsmen or dependants, made a foray against the wrongdoer, and swept away his cattle, and with them perhaps his wife and children, or he threatened him with supernatural penalties by 'fasting' upon him, as in the East even at the present day; or, finally, he reduced his adversary to servitude, or took his life." (*a*) There are only slight traces of this system of self-redress in the Roman Law of the time of Gaius and Justinian. Still there are sufficient to prove, conclusively, that the early history of Law was the same in Rome as elsewhere. When we apply ourselves to other systems of law which, from various causes, did not develop in the same manner as the Roman Law did—such, for

(*a*) *Justinian Insts.*, Ed. Moyle, vol. i., p. 614.

instance, as the Brehon Laws of Ireland, and the legal systems of Semitic nations—we find the system of private retaliation in full vigour, even in the most highly developed stage to which the law ever attained. There can be no doubt, also, that the primitive history of English Criminal Law was in this respect exactly the same. "The fact," says Mr. Justice Stephen, "that private vengeance of the person wronged by a crime was the principal source to which men trusted for the administration of criminal justice in early times, is one of the most characteristic circumstances connected with English Criminal Law, and has had much to do with the development of what may, perhaps, be regarded as its principal distinctive peculiarity, namely, the degree to which a criminal trial resembles a private litigation (*Hist. of Criminal Law*, i. 245). The development of both the English and Roman systems has, in a great measure, obliterated the traces of this system of primitive retaliation; and it is difficult to trace in them the various steps of the progress to a mature system of law. It is here that we invoke the aid of the other systems of law which I have mentioned. The Brehon Laws, arrested in their growth, at an early stage of legal development, by the unfortunate history of Ireland, throw a flood of light upon the early history of Penal Law, and supply us with the missing link of legal history. They exhibit to us, flourishing in full vigour, institutions and methods of procedure, of which only very slight traces remain in the Roman Law, and the very remembrance of which has been almost entirely lost in our own more perfect system of Criminal Law.

The primitive method for the redress of wrongs was, as I have said, simple retaliation upon the person of the wrongdoer. At this stage of human progress, *Law*, in any sense in which we use the term, cannot be said to have existed. It would be absurd to call savage retaliation Law; still this system of retaliation is the germ from which Penal Law has gradually developed itself; and we can, by comparing the laws of different nations at different periods of their development, actually trace the stages by which the practice of retaliation became transformed into a regular system of Criminal Law. The first stage in this progress was the growth of a custom for the injured person to accept some pecuniary satisfaction in lieu of his right of vengeance. The wrongdoer might thus buy off the revenge which he dreaded, if he chose to do so. This was, at first, a purely voluntary matter on both sides. There was no compulsion whatsoever. It lay entirely in the discretion of the injured person whether he would accept pecuniary satisfaction or wreak his vengeance on the wrongdoer. And the latter, if he were strong enough, could safely defy his enemy, and refuse to give any satisfaction. It was altogether a matter of private bargaining ; the injured man, according to his power, and according to the fierceness of his anger, exacting whatever sum he could from the wrongdoer. Gradually, however, a regular scale of payment was established—at first, for slight injuries, and then, afterwards, for more serious offences. Custom has enormous force among uncivilized nations. Men, naturally, and without any constraint, were satisfied to accept the same compensation as others in similar positions had been content with. Still there was no compulsion—no constraint whatsoever—and no intervention of any judicial authority.

It must not be forgotten that the right of personal revenge was also in many cases a duty. A man was bound by all the force of religion and custom to avenge the death of his kinsman. This duty was by universal practice imposed upon the nearest male relative—the avenger of blood, as he is called in the Scripture accounts. Among most nations, murder, like any other offence, could be compounded for between the wrongdoer and the nearest relative of the slain. We never hear of the death fine in historical times in Greece, but in Homer it is referred to more than once. Thus, in the 9th Book of the Iliad, Ajax, in reproaching Achilles for not accepting the offer of reparation made to him by Agamemnon, reminds him that even a brother's death may be appeased by a pecuniary fine, and that the murderer, having paid the fine, may remain at home among his own people free. One of the scenes said to have been depicted on the shield of Achilles is a dispute about a death fine. Among the ancient Germans the custom prevailed universally. Tacitus tells us that atonement was made for homicide by a certain number of cattle, and that by that means the whole family was appeased. By the *Lex Salica* the fine was paid in money, and varied according to the rank, sex, and age of the murdered person. (*a*) The early English laws were based on the same principle: the fine for homicide is constantly referred to in the Laws of Edgar and Athelstan. In Sweden the death fine was also recognized by the name *kinbote*, as a compensation for homicide. In the Roman Law there is no trace of it, so far as I am aware; but the provision of the Twelve Tables regarding homicide has not been preserved to us; and it is only from an incidental reference, many centuries later, that we learn that death was the penalty imposed for the crime. It is possible that, as in the case of lesser injuries, primitive Roman Law allowed a murderer to compound for his offence by a money payment; but it is more probable, I think, that the law regarded the life of a Roman citizen as too sacred to be atoned for by money payment. Among Semitic nations the death fine was very general, and it continued to prevail in the Turkish Empire down to our own day; but the acceptance of a death penalty was distinctly forbidden to the Jews by the Mosaic legislation. The life of a man was considered too sacred to be atoned for by money. (*b*) Religious influence had much to do everywhere, as we shall see, with the development of Criminal Law.

The death fine was, of course, a most important matter in cases where it was permitted to be paid and received, and it is in reference to it that a dispute would naturally arise: firstly, because its amount would necessarily be larger than that for lesser injuries; and, secondly, because the acceptance of too small a fine would naturally be looked upon as an evasion of his duty by the avenger of blood. The latter might accept a

(*a*) See *Lex Salica*, edited by Hessels & Kerr. Titles 14, 24, 35, 41–45.

(*b*) See Numbers xxxv. 31.

fine, but he could not, without disgrace, accept any small compensation for the death of his kinsman.

The first germ of any judicial proceeding is to be found in the settlement of the amount of these fines by the tribal assembly, which was held periodically among most primitive nations. Each party would naturally appeal to it, and probably in early times its principal work was the settlement of such disputes. At first the settlement was only suggested, neither party being bound by the decision; and it was not, apparently, for a very long period that any attempt was made to enforce decrees as to the amount of the fines. Where both parties were willing to refer the matter to the assembly, the decision of the latter was of course binding, and gradually it came to be usual and customary to do so.

We have, in English Law, very little trace of such a system as that which I have endeavoured to describe, but the Brehon Laws give us an exact picture of this state of society; and there can be little doubt that it preceded, everywhere, the establishment of a regular judicial system.

In fixing the amount of the fine to be paid, the Tribal Assembly would naturally pay attention to the likelihood of the injured person being satisfied with its decision. Thus the feelings of the aggrieved party, rather than the moral guilt of the offender, or even the amount of damage inflicted, was the primary matter which regulated the amount of the fine. At a later period, when law was fully developed, and the decisions of courts of justice regularly enforced, traces of this system remained in the rules regarding the penalty for different offences. The curious rule by which, according to Roman Law, a theft detected in the act was punished by a fine of twice the amount of that inflicted for a theft not so detected, is undoubtedly to be traced to this source. "The reason," says Mr. Poste, "why *furtum manifestum* was subjected to a heavier penalty than *furtum nec manifestum*, was not because the barbarous legislator supposed that detection in the act was an aggravation of the offence, but because he wished, by the amplitude of the legal remedy offered, to induce the aggrieved party not to take the law into his own hands and inflict summary vengeance on the offender." (*a*)

The Roman Law only exhibits, incidentally as it were, traces of the existence of such customs; but the Brehon Laws exhibit the system in full operation. The *Book of Aicill* mentions with great detail the various circumstances which are to be taken into account in fixing the amount of fines; and instances are recorded where injured persons refused, for various reasons, to accept the amount fixed.

How then did this purely voluntary system become transformed into a regularly enforced code of Penal Law? There can be little doubt that the enforced payment of the fines was a matter of gradual development. The Brehon Law tracts, for instance, contain no provision whatsoever for the enforcement of the fines, so that we are much puzzled to know what obligation there was on anyone to pay. We may conjecture that when first tribal assemblies or kings began to decide disputes authoritatively, they gave (if the wrongdoer were present) such assistance as was necessary to the complainant in exacting the punishment imposed. If the wrongdoer did not attend, there was, so far as we can learn, no means of compelling him to do so; but the principle of retaliation was again invoked here. He who refused to obey the law was deprived of its benefits. If any man refused to pay the fine imposed upon him by law for any offence, he was declared henceforth incapable of recovering fines for offences against himself. In other words, he was outlawed. There can be little doubt that outlawry was the first punishment imposed by society. The more archaic a body of law is the more minute are its provisions regarding outlawry. Such is the conclusion at which Sir H. Maine arrives:—"The earliest penalty for disobedience to the court was probably outlawry. The man who would not abide by its sentence went out of the law. If he were killed,

(*a*) Poste's *Gaius*, p. 460.

his kinsmen were forbidden, or were deterred by all the force of primitive opinion, from taking that vengeance which otherwise would have been their duty and their right." (*a*) The introduction of the system of outlawry is extremely important in that it marks the real origin of Criminal Law. In ancient law there is no such thing as a *crime*. The word *crimen* (connected with the Greek κρίνειν) is of comparatively modern origin in Roman Law, and necessarily implies a judicial proceeding of some kind.

Criminal Law, as distinct from *Penal* Law, involves some element of public condemnation—such was a sentence of outlawry. The right of vengeance, or the penalty paid and accepted in lieu of it, is a matter more of private than of public law. The term "*pœna*" does not, like "*crimen*," involve anything of a public nature. "There can be little doubt that the term '*pœna*' originally meant not so much penalty as composition for injury; the earliest *pœnæ* were sums in consideration of which the injured person consented to forego his customary right of self-redress, and the penal sums recovered by the plaintiff in a Roman action on *delict* attest the nature of the practice, though in them the 'penalty' is usually fixed by the State, and not by the parties." (*b*)

The prototype of a modern criminal trial appears in the solemn proclamation at the tribe meeting, after full inquiry of the sentence of outlawry. In Iceland the sentence was pronounced at the *Althing* by the Law man. In the Saga of Gisli the outlaw, (*c*) we have an account of the manner in which sentence of outlawry was passed in that country. Gisli in a quarrel had slain his opponent. He flies, and is pursued by Bork the Stout, brother of the slain man. "The next thing that happens is that Gisli sends word to his brothers-in-law, Helgi, and Sigurd, and Vestgen, to go to the Thing

(*a*) See his chapter on "The King in his relation to early civil justice," in *Early Law and Custom*, pp. 170–174.

(*b*) Moyle, *Insts. of Justinian*, vol. i., p. 616.

(*c*) "The Story of Gisli the Outlaw." Ed. by Sir G. Dasent.

(*i.e.* local assembly held periodically) and offer an atonement for him that he might not be outlawed. So they set off for the Thing, the sons of Bjartmar, and could bring nothing to pass about the atonement; and men go so far as to say that they behaved very ill, so that they almost burst out into tears ere the suit was over. They were then very young; and Bork the Stout was so very wroth they could do nothing with him." In England it was, under the old law, necessary that a man should be solemnly called at four county courts (*a*) before the sentence of outlawry could be pronounced against him. In theory outlawry still exists in our law, though it has long since become obsolete in practice.

Such is a slight sketch of the manner in which Criminal or Penal Law appears to have originated in all legal systems. When we pass this initial stage we find that laws developed themselves differently in different countries, according to differing circumstances of government, occupation, and temperament of the people. Different acts became crimes under different systems, but the general principle which underlay all was the principle of revenge. Those acts have everywhere come to be regarded as crimes which in early times tended to provoke vengeance or retaliation. The judicial authority, either the king or tribal assembly, at first regulated the manner in which this vengeance was to be enforced, and the terms upon which it might be commuted. Individuals were constrained to obey by sentences of outlawry. Gradually, then, partly in order to repress disorder, and partly in consequence of the disappearance, for various reasons, of the system of pecuniary fines, a regular system of Criminal Law came into existence; the same acts being punished as offences as were formerly liable to fine or personal revenge. We thus see how completely different the early development of Criminal Law, as a matter of fact, was, from what, according to the principles of analytical jurisprudence, we might naturally suppose it to have been.

(*a*) The County Courts were, in all probability, a survival, among the Anglo-Saxons, of the periodical tribal assembly of the Teutonic nations.

If there be any portion of the law which, according to our modern notions, corresponds to the Austinian theory, it is the Criminal Law. There is no other branch of law where the command or prohibition is so distinct, or where the existence of the sanction so clearly appears; yet we find that Criminal Law originated, not in any command at all, but in the custom of retaliation, at a time when there was no such thing in existence as a sovereign body to issue a command, and no means of enforcing one were it issued.

LECTURE II.

ANCIENT IRISH LAW.

THE most instructive source which we possess for the study of ancient criminal jurisprudence is the Brehon Law of Ancient Ireland. "The very causes," as Sir Henry Maine says, "which have denied a modern history to the Brehon Law have given it a special interest of its own in our day through the arrest of its development." (*a*) The various compilations of Law are also valuable as the best source for the study of the early history of Ireland. Irishmen, however, almost alone of all nations of the earth, consider their national history unworthy of study. Consequently, little or no interest is taken in the Law Tracts from an historical point of view, while their value in reference to the study of comparative jurisprudence has been only recently recognised. "The Brehon Law," as Dr. Richey states, in the Preface to the third volume of the Law Tracts, "exhibits more completely than any other code the ideas of an early society, as to the whole body of acts included under the name of crimes and torts." Consequently, a study of primitive penal law will naturally begin with it.

The antiquity of a system of law in one sense of the word does not at all depend upon its date. The English Law of Alfred is ancient; while the Roman Law of Justinian, which was some centuries prior to it in time, is extremely modern.

(*a*) *Early History of Institutions*, Pref. p. viii.

The Irish Law, though much of it was written as late as the twelfth or thirteenth century, is extremely ancient; and the most archaic principles prevailed in it centuries after they had disappeared elsewhere.

The Irish had undoubtedly attained to a very considerable degree of civilization between the sixth and the eleventh centuries, and the study of law seems to have been very popular among them. Of the books mentioned in Cormac's Glossary, a work of the ninth century, all, with two exceptions, are law treatises. The *Senchus Mor* and the *Book of Aicill* are the chief authorities on law which have come down to us. The Introduction to the former states that it was completed nine years after the coming of St. Patrick into Ireland—that is about the year 441 A. D.;—and though Sir Henry Maine is sceptical as to its being of such an early date, the authority of almost all Irish Scholars, including the translators, is against him, while from internal evidence there can be little doubt that it was composed, at any rate, very little later. A considerable portion of the text has been found to be in verse, which clearly points to an origin anterior to writing, the versification being evidently intended to assist the memory.

The *Senchus Mor* was, according to the account given in the introduction, composed in the time of Laeghaire, son of Niall, King of Erin, when Theodosius was Monarch (aird rig) of the world. The occasion of its being compiled is thus stated:— "Laeghaire ordered his people to kill a man of Patrick's people; and Laeghaire agreed to give his own award to the person who should kill the man, that he might discover whether he might grant forgiveness for it." Nuada Derg, brother of Laeghaire, then slew Odhran, Patrick's charioteer. Patrick referred the matter "to the judgment of the royal poet of the Island of Erin, viz. Dubhthach Mac na Lugair," who pronounced judgment of death. "It is evil to kill by a foul deed; I pronounce the judgment of death, of death for his crime to every one who kills"; but although Nuada was executed Patrick obtained heaven for him.

"What is understood from the above decision which God revealed to Patrick," says the commentator, "is that it was a middle course between forgiveness and retaliation: for retaliation prevailed in Erin before Patrick, and Patrick brought forgiveness with him, *i.e.* Nuada was put to death for his crime, and Patrick obtained heaven for him. But there is forgiveness in that sentence, and there is also retaliation. At this day we keep between forgiveness and retaliation, for as at present no one has the power of bestowing heaven, as Patrick had that day, so no one is put to death for his intentional crimes as long as Eric fine is obtained; and whenever 'Eric fine' is not obtained he is put to death for his intentional crimes, and placed on the sea for his ignorant crimes and unlawful obstructions."

After this judgment, Laeghaire decides that all the laws should be settled and arranged in accordance with the spirit of the new religion. "It was then Dubhthach was ordered to exhibit the judgments and all the poetry of Erin, and every law which prevailed among the men of Erin, through the law of nature, and the law of the seers, and in the judgments of the island of Erin and in the poets," and "what did not clash with the Word of God in the written law and in the New Testament, and with the consciences of the believers, was confirmed in the laws of the Brehons by Patrick and by the ecclesiastics and the chieftains of Erin; for the law of nature had been quite right, except the faith and its obligations, and the harmony of the Church and the people. And this is the *Senchus Mor*."

Two points are especially to be noted in this account. In the first place, it distinctly recognises retaliation as the origin of penal law; and, in the second place, it identifies law with poetry, in a manner which appears extremely curious to the modern reader. The leading authority in legal matters is the Royal Poet, who exhibited the judgments "and all the poetry of Erin" to Patrick. This leads us at once to the conclusion that the work was originally compiled at a time when writing was unknown; and the extremely archaic character of the law in other respects confirms this view. There can be no doubt, indeed, that at whatever date the *Senchus Mor* was actually compiled, the contents of it had been handed down from a very remote period. There is no mention of coined money throughout the work; the measure of value is a "cumhal," which originally meant a female slave, and then her value, which was considered to be equivalent to that of three cows. Kinship is the basis of society. The land is chiefly owned in common, although separate ownership is not unknown. The family, and even the tribe, are responsible for the crimes of individuals; and all crimes are commuted by a money payment. The strangest thing of all about the *Senchus Mor*, as well as the other Law Tracts, is that, side by side with the most archaic principles, we find extremely modern doctrines on some subjects, the latter, in all probability, having been adopted from the Roman Law, and introduced at a later period as glosses to the original MSS. Minute regulations, for instance, are laid down as to contracts; and the provisions regarding fraud remind us forcibly of the very elastic *exceptio doli mali* of the Roman system. On the whole, however, the laws were just and equitable; hence the desire frequently shown by Norman or English settlers to adopt them—a tendency which it took all the energies of the Parliament of the Pale to counteract and repress.

The *Senchus Mor* became the leading authority on law throughout Ireland, and continued to be such as long as the Irish tribes retained their independence. Its authority did not completely cease until the seventeenth century. During all this period, of probably 1000 years, the law underwent little or no alteration. Various causes produced this result, the chief one being the unsettled condition of Ireland, and the absence of any strong central authority to alter or develop the legal system. Hence the extremely archaic character of the law, even in its latest development, and the interest which consequently attaches to it at the present day.

Anyone who is familiar with the history of Ireland will have little difficulty in explaining how it was that the law remained unchanged for such a long period. A strong central authority is the chief requisite for the development of a legal system, and such did not exist in Ireland at any time after the tenth century. The Danes destroyed the central monarchy which was creeping into existence at that time. Then the Normans came under Strongbow, backed up by Henry II. of England. They never completely subdued the country, but they were far too strong to be driven out. And, as Mr. Lecky so well expresses it, "the hostile power planted in the heart of the nation destroyed all possibility of central government, while it was itself incapable of fulfilling that function." (*a*) The absence of any authority to enforce or amend the law prevented its internal development, while foreign influence was in a great measure excluded by the intense hatred of the invaders, and the strong disinclination to adopt any of their institutions. Not a trace of English law is to be found in any of the Law Tracts.

The *Book of Aicill*, the second in importance of the Law Tracts, is taken up with that branch of law which we now call Criminal Law. But in the Ancient Irish Law there was no distinction between civil and criminal law, or rather, it would be more exact to say, there was no such thing as criminal law in existence. Self-redress was the one and only remedy recognised. All proceedings, whether for a crime, a tort, or a breach of contract, were identical in origin, and prosecuted in the same manner, namely, by levying a distress.

The learned editors of the Law Tracts, in the Introduction to the *Book of Aicill*, shortly summarize the principles of the law which it contains as follows :—"The features of early law in criminal matters, which come out with peculiar clearness in the Brehon Law Tracts, and especially in the present work, may be summed up as follows :—

"(1) The entire absence of any legislative or judicial power ; from which it follows—

(*a*) *History of England in the Eighteenth Century*, vol ii. p. 93.

"(2) That the law is purely customary, and theoretically incapable of alteration; and

"(3) That all judicial authority is purely consensual, and the judgments are merely awards founded upon a submission to arbitration, whose only sanction is public opinion;

"(4) That all the acts defined by us as crimes are classed as torts; and

"(5) That the form which all judgments assumed is an assessment of damages." (*a*)

All offences from murder or intentional homicide to the most trifling theft or insult were, under the Brehon Law, the subject of pecuniary compensation only. The offender, if he paid the stipulated sum, was entirely free from any punishment. If he was unable or unwilling to pay, the injured person might either levy a distress on his goods, or upon those of his near relatives, or exact vengeance in whatever way he thought right. The *Eric fine*, as it was called, forms the most prominent, and to the modern student by far the most interesting, feature of the Laws. The rules for calculating its amount were extremely complicated, and a great portion of the Law Tracts is taken up in discussing them. The proportions are most minutely laid down in which relatives of the offender were bound to pay, in case of the latter making default; the primitive idea of the responsibility of the tribe for the acts of its members being recognised generally throughout the laws.

The amount of the fine varied, partly according to the rank of the person injured, partly according to that of the offender, and partly according to the nature of the act. A double fine was due for homicide, where anger was shown, *i.e.* where probably there was what we would call "malice"; but even for an accidental or unintentional homicide, an Eric fine was imposed. Exemption from liability for an accidental injury is entirely a modern idea. All bodies of ancient law punish unintentional as well as intentional offences. Even in our own Criminal Law,

(*a*) Translator's Introduction to the *Book of Aicill*, p. lxxxix.

what we now call excusable homicide was not entirely free from punishment until a very recent date.

The amount of the Eric fines varied, as I have said, according to the rank of the person killed; being highest in the case of a chief or a bishop, and next in the case of a poet. It was paid to the relatives of the deceased person in the proportion in which they were entitled to inherit his property. Different names are used in the laws for the fines, and there is some confusion as to the mode of calculating the amount. The terms coirpdire (coirpdire), einaclann (enachlan), and eiric (eric), are used indiscriminately. The einaclann or "honour-price," as it is translated, was the price at which a man's life was assessed. Whether it was equivalent to the eiric, or was a separate payment, it is impossible to say. The amount of the honour-price depended on either wealth, family, or profession, and a man was allowed to elect by which it should be calculated; but having once made his election he was bound by it for ever. Some passages in the Laws assume that a king or chief might elect to base his honour-price on the amount of his possessions. This is an extremely interesting fact, as showing that the great importance of wealth is not, as is generally supposed, peculiar to modern society.

The assessment of damages varying in this way became extremely complicated. If injuries were committed by both sides they could be set off against each other, so that if a feud had been going on for any lengthened period between two families, the legal proceedings which resulted resembled the taking of an account in equity rather than a criminal trial.

The custom of punishing homicide and other crimes by a fine was common to all ancient systems of law. Everywhere there are traces of it; but in general it disappeared at such an early period in the development of the law, that we can learn little as to the way in which it originally sprung up. In Ireland, on the other hand, the law was, from various causes, stereotyped in its original form, and remained unchanged throughout the whole course of its history, so that this ancient custom continued to prevail here centuries after it had disappeared elsewhere. Thus when an English Deputy, during the reign of Elizabeth, informed Mac Guire of Fermanagh that he must admit a sheriff into his territory, the Irish chief replied that the sheriff should be welcome, but at the same time inquired the amount of his "Eric," that in case anybody should cut off his head he might levy it upon the country. To allow such a serious crime as murder to be commuted by a money payment was certainly an indication of barbarism, and this probably contributed in a great degree to prevent the establishment of order throughout the native portion of Ireland. The English writers who denounced the custom of Eric fines as "wicked" and "damnable," were probably unaware that a similar custom originally prevailed in every country of Europe, including their own. Still there is a considerable amount of truth, though some exaggeration, in the remark of Davis, that "the people which doth use it, must of necessity be rebelles to all good government, destroy the commonwealth wherein they live, and bring barbarism and desolation upon the richest and most fruitful land of the world." The continuance of such a custom would effectually prevent any real social progress in the nation. "It cannot be doubted," as Dr. Richey remarks, "that to a persistent adherence to the idea of compensation atoning for injury, and to a want of perception of the criminality of any act, much of the disorder and lawlessness apparently inherent in the Irish Celtic tribes must be attributed." (*a*)

The fine for homicide being thus such a very archaic institution, if we could ascertain the way in which it originated we would probably learn the origin of law itself. The account given of the Eric fine in the Brehon Laws, and the references to it in the historical tales of the Ancient Irish, materially assist us in this inquiry. The origin of law is stated by Sir Henry Maine to have been in all cases a voluntary submission to arbitration. This theory is based upon the forms of the *legis actio sacramenti* of the Romans, as described by Gaius, and has been

(*a*) Introduction to *Brehon Laws*, vol. iii. p. 122.

confirmed by many indications in other systems of law; but the Brehon Laws show us that there was a stage anterior even to that of arbitration; and this we learn, not from any indistinct indications of it in the procedure of a more fully developed system, but from contemporary references, and from the provisions of the laws themselves. We stand here, it may be fairly said, on the very threshold of law, and we are enabled to see how it arose in a state of society where anarchy and disorder had previously prevailed. The theory that the system of pecuniary fines immediately succeeded the custom of mere retaliation, which is considered probable by Sir Henry Maine, is completely confirmed by the accounts given of the Eric fines in the Brehon Laws, and in the historical tales of the Ancient Irish Celts. But how did the fine come to take the place of retaliation? This we shall see from the way in which the fine was itself originally regarded. The payment is invariably treated in the laws as a satisfaction to the injured party for his surrender of his right of revenge, and when the fine is not paid, the right of revenge revives as of course.

In very early times the acceptance of the fine was even optional; the injured person if he preferred to revenge himself on his adversary might do so freely. A story contained in the *Book of Lecain* illustrates this stage of legal progress. It is called the "Fate of the Children of Turenn," and is of very ancient date, being referred to in Cormac's *Glossary*, a work of the ninth or tenth century. The father of Luga, a powerful warrior, had been slain by the children of Turenn. Luga, after celebrating the funeral rites, addresses his followers in the following terms:—

"Go ye now to Tara, where the King of Erin sits on his throne with the Dedannans around him; but do not make these things known till I myself have told them."

"So Luga's people went straightway to Tara, as he had bade them; but of the murder of Kian they said naught. Luga himself arrived some time after, and was received with great honour, being put to sit high over the others at the King's side; for the fame of his mighty deeds at the battle of the Assembly Plain had been noised over the whole country, and had come to the ears of the King.

"After he was seated, he looked round the hall, and saw the sons of Turenn in the assembly. Now these three sons of Turenn exceeded all the champions in Tara, in comeliness of person, in swiftness of foot, and in feats of arms; and, next to Luga himself, they were the best and bravest in the battles against the Formorians; wherefore they were honoured by the King beyond most others.

"Luga asked the King that the chain of silence should be shaken; and when all were listening in silence, he stood up and spoke:—

"'I perceive ye nobles of the Dedannan race that you have given me your attention, and now I have a question to put to each man here present: what vengeance would you take of the man who should knowingly and of design kill your father?'

"They were all struck with amazement on hearing this, and the King of Erin said:—

"'What does this mean? For that your father has not been killed, this we all know well!'

"'My father has indeed been killed,' said Luga, 'and I see now here in this hall those who slew him. And furthermore, I know the manner in which they put him to death, even as they know it themselves.'

"The sons of Turenn hearing all this said nothing; but the King spoke aloud and said:—'If any man should wilfully slay my father, it is not in one hour or one day I would have him put to death; but I would lop off one of his members each day, till I saw him die in torment under my hands.' All the nobles said the same, and the sons of Turenn in like manner.

"'The persons who slew my father are here present, and are joining with the rest in this judgment,' said Luga; 'and as the Dedannans are all now here to witness, I claim that the three who have done this evil deed shall pay me a fitting Eric fine for my father. Should they refuse, I shall not indeed transgress the King's law, nor violate his protection; but of a certainty they shall not leave this Hall of Micorta till the matter is settled.'

"And the King of Erin said:—'If I had killed your father, *I should be well content if you were willing to accept an Eric fine from me.*'

"Now the sons of Turenn spoke amongst themselves, and Ur and Urcar said:—'It is of us Luga speaks this speech. He has doubtless found out that we slew his father; and it is better that we now acknowledge the deed, for it will avail us naught to hide it.'"

Brian, however, at first set his face against this, saying that he feared Luga only wanted an acknowledgment from them in presence of the other Dedannans, and that afterwards he might not accept a fine. But the other two were earnest in pressing him, so that he consented, and then he spoke to Luga:—

"'It is of us thou speakest these things, Luga; for it has been said that we three have been at enmity with the three sons of Canta. Now as to the slaying of thy father Kian, let that matter rest; but we are willing to pay an Eric fine for him, even as if we had killed him.'

"'I shall accept an Eric fine from you,' said Luga, 'though ye indeed fear I shall not. I shall now name before this assembly the fine I ask, and if you think it too much, I shall take off a part of it.'

He then names the fine, and the story proceeds. (*a*)

We see from this interesting anecdote that a voluntary submission to arbitration was not the first stage in the development of law, but that there was a stage earlier even than this, namely—that of an ordinary agreement or bargain between the parties, settling the amount of the damages. The fine is not imposed by any recognised authority. The King claims no jurisdiction in the matter. He does not even suggest the amount of

(*a*) The full tale, text and translation, is published by O'Curry in the *Atlantis*. It is referred to in Cormac's *Glossary* (about A.D. 900). The whole story is contained in the *Book of Lecain* (about 1416 A.D.).

the fine—a matter which the parties settle between themselves. One of them has suffered a wrong, and demands to be paid compensation, as the price of his renouncing his right to revenge. He appeals to those around to say whether what he asks is fair compensation; and they merely give their opinion, without attempting to arbitrate or interfere in the matter in any way.

We are here at a much earlier stage of law than that which is exhibited in the fictitious *legis actio sacramenti* of the Romans. There is no command to the parties to desist, corresponding to the *mittite ambo hominem.* The injured person merely demands compensation, and it is perfectly optional with him to take it or not. The primitive right to retaliation has not yet disappeared, nor is there any moral or legal restraint on its exercise, provided the peace or protection of another is not violated thereby. The progress of the law from this beginning is not difficult to conjecture. If the parties could not agree as to the amount of the damages, nothing would be more natural than that it should be referred to the poet or Brehon who attended the chief of the tribe, to decide. His duty was to recite the history of the tribe at the various tribal gatherings, and he would consequently be able to say what had been given and accepted in similar cases. If either party, after having agreed to submit the matter to him, refused to abide by his decision, such breach of faith would naturally be severely condemned by the whole tribe, and means would probably be taken to inflict punishment. In this way a regular legal system would spring up.

Although in the legal action described by Gaius, the idea of law has been much more fully developed than here, still we find in an earlier period of the Roman Law, a striking parallel to the Irish Eric fine. The fragments of the Twelve Tables which remain contain no provision regarding homicide, but the punishment for bodily injuries is specified, and ancient law invariably deals with these in the same way as with homicide. The words of the Eighth Table are, *si membrum rupit, ni cum eo pacit talio esto*—"Retaliation against him who breaks the limb of another and does not offer compensation." Now if the words *talio esto* mean, as I presume they may, "let the injured person retaliate," we are precisely at the same stage as that which the story of the children of Turenn displays to us in the Irish Law. In the case of homicide indeed we are informed by Pliny that death was the punishment inflicted by the Twelve Tables; but it is not a very extravagant conjecture to assume that the *talio esto* was qualified in the same way in this case as in the other. The law in Mahommedan countries is in general based on entirely different principles from those prevailing in Europe, yet strange to say we find there also an exact parallel to the Eric fine. Mr. Sale tells us, in a note to the second chapter of the Koran, that it is a common practice in Mahommedan countries, particularly in Persia, when a man is murdered, that the relations of the deceased should have their choice, either to have the murderer put into their hands to be put to death, or to accept a pecuniary satisfaction. Here we have a striking confirmation of the theory that Penal Law originated everywhere in the system of buying off revenge by the payment of a sum of money.

The close connexion between the Eric fine and private revenge explains also the singular custom of levying the fine on the relations of the murderer, if the latter absconded or was unable to pay. Those who seek vengeance are not over-scrupulous as to the persons upon whom they inflict it; and the revenge would naturally be directed in the first instance against the relatives of the wrongdoer. It is their interest then to buy it off, both in order to save themselves and to protect one of their number. Hence when the custom becomes a law, the fine is levied not alone upon the person who is morally guilty, but on his innocent relatives as well. If the fine was paid, a promise was made not to further seek vengeance, and the bargain was complete. In the case of an habitual criminal, the family could relieve themselves from responsibility for his acts by formally expelling him from their body. Probably this was a provision introduced into the laws at a somewhat late period.

The liability of the family to pay the fine for the offence of one of its members was always regarded as reciprocal to its right to receive it in case such member was himself killed. The law contained provisions as to priority of payment corresponding to the rules of succession to property on death. The fine was leviable in the first instance on the criminal himself, then on his sons, then on his father, then on his "deirb-fine" (a class of relations, the limits of which are not precisely known), then, passing beyond the range of the family, on any person who harboured or assisted him, and finally on the King. If his relations were compelled to pay the fine they had naturally the right to compensate themselves out of his property, and his share in the land held in common was forfeited. The family could also relieve themselves from responsibility for the acts of an habitual criminal, by formally expelling him from their body, and paying a fine to the King and certain other persons, as a composition for any future crimes he might commit.

The custom of levying the fine upon the whole tribe to which the murderer belongs is, as I have said, easily explained on the principle of retaliation. In a tribal society, an injury inflicted by one member of a tribe on a stranger naturally brings down vengeance on the whole tribe to which he belongs. There is no such responsibility, however, for the acts of a stranger living under the protection of the tribe, provided he is given up to the vengeance of those whom he has injured. We have an account in the *Senchus Mor* (Introduction, p. 71) of a "Leading Case" on this point. A chief, driven from his own country for his depredations, took refuge with Fergus, King of Uladh, who received him under his protection. After awhile he set out "to go to his own tribe to demand justice from them, but was met and killed by five members of the tribe, one of whom was the son of a stranger." Fergus went with forces from the North to demand satisfaction, and justice was deeed to him, *i. e.* three times seven cumhals (*a*)—seven cumhals

(*a*) A "cumhal" was the value of a female slave, generally considered to be equivalent to three oxen.

of gold, and seven of silver, and land of seven cumhals for the crime of the five natives; and Dora, the daughter of Buidhe, was given as a pledge for the crime of her son, for he was the son of a stranger, and was begotten against the wish of, or without the knowledge of, the tribe of the mother. (*a*) After this Fergus made a perfect covenant respecting this Eric fine, and returned to his own country, having his bondmaid with him in bondage.

The liability of the tribe appears from this case to have been strictly confined to its own members. For strangers there was no responsibility, if they were deprived of protection after they committed an offence, and given up for punishment. The *noxæ deditio* of the Roman Law is here very forcibly suggested to us.

Theft was punished by fine in the same way as homicide, but it was lawful to kill a thief who was unknown, if there was no power of arresting him at the time of his committing the offence. If he were arrested, and if he or his relations were able to pay fines, they were obliged to compensate not only the owner of the stolen property, but a number of other persons who were considered to be injured by the offence. "The fine for stealing from a house is a difficult fine," says the *Book of Aicill* (p. 459). "A fine was due to the owner of the house for violation of his precinct, to the occupant of the room from which the stolen article was taken, and also a fine to seven nobles or chiefs of companies who were in the habit of enjoying the hospitality of the house."

In one respect the Brehon Law was extremely modern in its view of crime. An attempt was considered equivalent to the actual commission of the deed. This is probably one of the cases in which the Irish lawyers borrowed from the Civil Law "Dolus pro facto accipitur," being the rule regarding

(*a*) A female member of the tribe marrying out of it lost all her rights, and her children were regarded as strangers. The rule in the Hebrew Law was the same. A daughter could not marry out of her tribe without forfeiting her inheritance. (See Numb. xxxvi. 6, 7.)

homicide in that system. The intention was itself a crime, and punished by a separate fine, if it was clearly evidenced by an overt act. Thus, if a man went to kill one person and killed another by mistake, a fine for the intention was due to him whom it was intended to kill, even though no injury was done to him, in addition to that due to the friends of the murdered man.

"The general impression," says Dr. Richey, "produced by the rules in the commentary is that the attempt to commit an act was treated as equivalent to its commission, unless the results of the attempt were very insignificant. Thus, if an attempt were made to slay, or to inflict an injury which would endure for life, and blood were shed, the fine was the same as if the attempt had succeeded; if the injury did not amount to the shedding of blood the fine was reduced to one-half. If the intention were to inflict any specified injury, and a different injury was inflicted, a calculation was made of the total of 'a seventh for intention, one-half for going to the place, and the body fine for inflicting the wound,' and the plaintiff could elect between the result of this calculation and the fine for the wound he intended to inflict and the fine for the wound he actually inflicted." (*a*)

The judicial functions of the King are recognised in the Brehon Law as in all other systems of ancient jurisprudence. A false judging King is frequently mentioned as one worthy of punishment. The account given in the commencement of the *Book of Aicill* of the composition of that work shows the important position occupied by a King in judicial matters. King Cormac having been accidentally wounded at Temhair was obliged to abdicate his sovereignty. "It was a prohibited thing that one with a blemish should be King at Temhair. And Cormac was therefore sent out to be cured to Aicill, close to Temhair; and Temhair could be seen from Aicill, but Aicill could not be seen from Temhair. And

(*a*) Introduction to *Book of Aicill.* p. cix.

the sovereignty of Erinn was given to Coirpri Lifechair, son of Cormac; and in every difficult case of judgment that came to him he used to go and ask his father about it; and his father used to say to him, 'My son, that thou mayest know,' and explain to him 'the exemptions' " (*a*).

The King, though he could declare the law, had no power to alter it. His function was merely, as chief of the tribal assembly, to see that the proper customs were observed. The Royal justice which under the English system gradually superseded all others in criminal matters did not exist in Ireland.

Curiously enough, however, we find in the Brehon Law the very same germ from which Royal justice sprang in England, though it never had time or opportunity to develop itself in the Irish system. The violation of the King's Peace was the original offence from which the jurisdiction of the Sovereign in criminal matters has gradually grown in English Law. Such, at least, is the opinion of one of our ablest living authorities on legal matters, Sir Frederick Pollock. I take the following note from his Essay on "The History of English Law as a branch of Politics":—

"The technical use of 'The King's peace' is, I suspect, connected with the very ancient rule that a breach of the peace in a house must be atoned for in proportion to the householder's rank. If it was in the King's dwelling, the offender's life was in the King's hands. This peculiar sanctity of the King's house was gradually extended to all persons who were about his business, or specially under his protection; but when the Crown undertook to keep the peace everywhere, the King's peace became coincident with the general peace of the kingdom, and his especial protection was deemed to be extended to all peaceable subjects. In substance the term marks the establishment of the conception of public justice, exercised on behalf of the whole commonwealth, as something apart from and above the right of private vengeance—a right which the

(*a*) *Book of Aicill, Ancient Laws of Ireland*, vol. iii., p. 85.

party offended might pursue or not, or accept compensation for, as he thought fit" (*a*).

A similar rule prevailed under the Brehon Law protecting the sanctity of a man's dwelling and the district around it, and punishing by a fine any act of violence committed there by a stranger. In the case of theft, we have already seen that a fine was due not only to the owner of the stolen property, but also to the owner of the house in which the theft was committed, for the violation of his "precinct." The householder had a similar right in case any other offence was committed within the prescribed limits. The Irish word (maigin) translated "precinct," meant a portion of land lying round the house of a chief or other dignitary. The territorial limits of this right are minutely specified in the laws, and varied according to rank. Within this "precinct" the owner of the house had a right to prevent acts of violence, lest probably he or his property should be injured thereby. The early English law contained similar rules; the "tûn" corresponding to the "maighin." Thus, by the laws of Æthelred, if one man killed another within the King's tûn, he should make bōt, 50 shillings, and within an earl's tûn, 12 shillings. The mode in which the limit of the maighin was calculated proves its object; the smallest limit was the distance to which a spear could be thrown from the door, and that for the higher ranks was some multiple of this. The distance to which a spear could be thrown was the natural limit to the possibility of danger to the house or its occupant from the quarrel. Modern international law furnishes us with an exact parallel. A maritime league from the shore of a neutral territory is considered the furthest distance to which a cannon-shot can carry; and an act of war within this limit is considered a violation of the rights of the neutral power in consequence of the danger to which it exposes the persons and property of its subjects. This is only one of the many cases in which ancient private law resembles modern international law.

(*a*) *Essays on Jurisprudence and Ethics*, p. 205 (note).

The tract on Precincts (maigne), contained in the fourth volume of the *Ancient Laws of Ireland*, lays down the following rules for calculating the extent of the precinct:—"The spear measures twelve fists between its iron head and the place where the horn is put upon its extremity, *i.e.* the extremity of its handle. Now, the shot of this which the bo-aire chief casts as he sits in the door of his house is the extent of the inviolable precinct of the bo-aire chief respecting his 'seds;' and the 'aire-desa' chief has twice this extent; and every grade from that up to the king of a territory has double it, *i.e.* the king of a territory has sixty-four shots as the extent of his inviolable precinct. And it is by the 'green' these shots are measured for every inviolable precinct; and where they are discharged from is from the place where they (the parties) constantly sit.

"A King of Kings: it is he that has Kings, *i.e.* the King of a province, and the King of Erin, and also the 'co-arb' of Patrick (*a*); as far as their 'scor' lands (*b*) extend on every side, that is their inviolable precinct."

The large extent of the King's precinct made every offence committed within his territory an offence against him if he chose so to regard it. Had the Irish sovereigns succeeded in attaining to the same power and supremacy as the Anglo-Saxon monarchs, a system of Royal justice would probably have sprung up in Ireland as it did in England, but unfortunately this never happened.

The Brehon Law appears, indeed, to have been at one time on the point of attaining to the position of a code of rules enforced by a sanction—not a sanction of a religious or supernatural nature, as is suggested by Sir Henry Maine (*c*), but one suggested by this very principle of retaliation, which was the basis of the whole Penal Law, namely, outlawry. The Brehon Law in this, as in so many other points, gives us, I think, a correct illustration of the growth of law in all ancient communities. The right to receive fines was always correlative

(*a*) The Archbishop of Armagh. (*b*) Plain, or meadow lands.

(*c*) *Early History of Institutions*, p. 37.

with the duty of paying them. The persons who were entitled to receive the fine in the case of the death of any individual, were those on whom the onus of paying would have fallen if that individual had committed a crime himself. He who refuses, however, to bear the burden is not entitled to partake of the benefit of the law; and so we find that where a crime was committed, for which Eric fine was not paid, the criminal was permanently deprived of his right to honour-price. This was tantamount to outlawry—an exceedingly severe sentence in a disturbed condition of society. The life of the criminal was then at the mercy of anyone who bore enmity towards him, or who had any interest in his death. "The life of every law-breaker is fully forfeited," says the *Book of Aicill.* "There are four dignitaries of a territory," says the *Senchus Mór*, "who may be degraded: a false-judging king, a stumbling bishop, a fraudulent poet, an unworthy chieftain who does not fulfil his duties. *Dire-fine is not due to them.*"

The commentary which follows this latter passage was in all probability written at a much later period; it deals not only with the more serious crimes for which the whole of the honour-price was forfeited at once, but also with lesser offences, on account of which a part only was taken away, unless the offence was repeated, thus:—

"False judgment, and false witness, and false testimony, and fraudulent pledging, and false proof, and false information, and false character-giving, and bad word, and bad story, and lying in general, whether in the case of the Church or the laity—every one of these deprives the man who is guilty of such of half his honour-price up to the third time, but it does not deprive him with regard to all until the third time, and it takes away even this half honour-price from everyone from the third time out. And he may lose this half honour-price by a different person; and he thus loses full honour-price with respect to the latter person, or with respect to the person against whom he had committed the first injury. Theft or eating stolen food in the house of one of any grade, or having stolen food in it constantly ; and treachery, and fratricide, and secret murder—each of these deprives a person of his full honour-price at once."

This system of depriving persons of honour-price, either wholly or partially for offences, marks a completely new epoch in the law. Society now for the first time intervenes in the matter. We pass at once from the era of torts to that of crimes. The true difference between a tort and a crime lies in the remedy, not in the nature of the act. All injuries are offences against individuals, and all more or less cause alarm and apprehension amongst others, lest they should suffer in the same way. But in some cases the remedy is left in the hands of the individual wronged, in others the State imposes the penalty. In the first case we speak of the offence as a tort ; in the latter as a crime. This deprivation of honour-price was probably proclaimed at a tribal meeting. There is no reference indeed, so far as I know, in the Irish law to anything like a public trial; still, some passages manifestly imply it. Entire exemption from fine, for instance, is allowed in the *Book of Aicill* to a person who kills "a condemned outlaw."

Outlawry thus appears to have been the primitive *punishment* as distinct from revenge imposed for crimes. The Irish Law is, in this, as in other cases, a type of primitive usage generally. The early English Law was similar, allowing no fine or compensation to relatives in case of the murder of an outlaw, "for that he resisted God's law or the King's;" and outlawry continued to be the chief punishment for crime in England until long after the Conquest. A great portion of Bracton's treatise, *De Corona*, is taken up with the matter—a fact which shows what an important position it occupied as a punishment in his time.

It is only necessary to consider, for a moment, the position of an outlaw in a chronically disturbed state of society in order to estimate the severity of this punishment. Suppose, for instance, he had been banished from his family, and that his tribe had deprived him of his honour-price, and declared that no dire-fine should be payable for his murder; he might then have been killed with impunity by any person, or any body of persons who had any motive for doing so. His only chance was to gain the "protection" of some powerful chief. As, however, anyone who sheltered him became liable for his acts, few would be willing to receive him; and if he escaped with his life, he became, practically, a slave to his protector, who was entitled to Eric fine if he killed him, and liable for his acts if he committed any crime. It is more than probable that the class of "fuidhir" tenants, frequently referred to in the laws, was composed mainly of these lawless men who had fled from other tribes on account of their crimes. Their position was one of great misery. They were altogether at the mercy of their lords, and liable to whatever rent he might demand for any land they occupied. This is the class, most probably, referred to by English writers of the seventeenth century, when they speak of the Irish chiefs rack-renting their tenantry, for the chief had no power to impose more than a "fair rent" on a member of his own tribe.

The study of the Brehon Law thus enables us to trace the progress of primitive ideas as to penal legislation generally. The earliest source to which we can trace back Penal Law is the principle of simple retaliation—an eye for an eye, a tooth for a tooth, life for life. This retaliation was not imposed, but simply permitted by society. The next step is the *custom* of buying off vengeance, either by the individual who has inflicted the injury, or his tribe. A pecuniary payment thus comes to be looked upon as a satisfaction for a crime. The wrong-doer gains his life: the injured man something valuable, in lieu of useless vengeance, his pride at the same time being appeased by the submission: society is benefited by an end being put to disturbance and fighting. Once the custom becomes general, disputes will certainly arise as to the amount of the payment. If the parties cannot come to terms both will lose; to avoid such a contingency they agree to refer it to the arbitration of the person who is most likely to know what was usually the amount paid in similar cases—this is the poet of the tribe, whose duty it is to recite its history at the tribal meetings. The ancient Irish Law expressly tells us that in former times the legal jurisdiction was vested in the poets. The next step is the direct intervention of the tribe itself, or its chief. The conduct of the man who refuses to submit his case to arbitration is plainly unreasonable. The whole tribe is interested in preserving peace—his conduct imperils it—they will therefore endeavour to force him to submit. The retaliative principle again recurs here. If he refuses to pay fines, what more natural than to refuse to allow him to recover them? His honour-price is forfeited, and thereby he at once becomes a "lawless man," whom anybody may kill with impunity. The prototype of a modern criminal trial then appears in the solemn proclamation at the tribal meeting, by the King or chief, of this sentence of outlawry. We have no direct evidence that the Brehon Law ever attained to this latter stage of development—at all events it never passed beyond it.

LECTURE III.

LAW OF SEMITIC RACES.

I.—HEBREW LAW.

FROM the study of the Ancient Irish Law, I pass at once to the consideration of another system of archaic jurisprudence, which illustrates in a remarkable manner the primitive history of Penal Law: namely, the Ancient Hebrew Law, as exhibited to us in the Books of the Old Testament. Like the Irish Law, it never developed into a regular system of criminal jurisprudence, but continued throughout its history to exhibit the same features of primitive usage as in its earliest origin. The non-progressive character of the law is, however, due to entirely different causes in the two cases. In Ireland it arose from the unsettled condition of the country, and the absence of a firm, settled government. Among the Jews it arose from the connexion between Law and Religion. Nothing so much checks the growth of Law in a community as the identification of it with religion. The recognition of the sacredness of rules of Law naturally offers a very strong obstacle to alteration of any kind in them. Nothing has so much facilitated legal progress among European nations as the fact that the religion of all of them is derived from a foreign source. A native religion naturally becomes identified with Law and retards progress; but religious precepts taken from a foreign source, on the other hand, by offering an ideal of morality to which the law seeks to attain, assist very materially in the improvement and development of the Law. The Decalogue, that "smallest, but oldest and most important of all works of law," as it is called by Ewald (*a*), has materially assisted the growth of English Criminal Law, by affording a succinct and definite code of morality, which it is the true aim of all law to apply and enforce. It proclaims its divine origin, by the comprehensive manner in which it deals with the most important of all matters to society and to the individual, the observance of religion, filial piety, the protection of life, of chastity, of property, and of civil security; while the concluding commandment, which contains merely a general prohibition of the mental state which leads to the transgression of the others, binds together the moral and legal elements in one comprehensive whole, and thus forms a fitting close to a code, so far in advance of any moral or religious ideas of the time, that we are constrained to acknowledge its divine origin.

Among Eastern nations, where ideas of progress scarcely exist, primitive customs usually acquire the same sanctity as moral and religious precepts, and thus the law, instead of being assisted, is retarded in its development by the influence of religion. Such was the case with the Jews. The following incident, mentioned by Mr. C. P. Ilbert, C.S.I., in an interesting article on Indian Codification, recently published in the "Law Quarterly Review" (vol. v., p. 367), shows the tenacity with which the Jews still cling to their primeval customs. "Some time in the year 1886," he says, "I received a deputation from the Jews of Aden, asking that they might be exempted from the operation of the Indian Succession Act (X. of 1865). That Act applied to the Jews of British India, a small class of persons. Aden is technically part of British India. Therefore the Act applied to the Jews of Aden. But for some twenty years the Jews of Aden remained in blissful ignorance of its existence. At last a case raising a question of succession among Aden Jews found its way into the Civil Court at Aden.

(*a*) *History of Israel*, vol. ii., p. 162.

The Judge looked up his law, and found that the Succession Act regulated the case. His decision fluttered the community, and they asked that they might be restored to their old law. On inquiring what that law was I was referred to a passage in the Book of Numbers (xxvii. 1-11), containing what may without profanity be called the ruling in Zelophehad's case. The text lays down the rule of succession to be observed when an Israelite dies leaving daughters, but no son. My Aden friends told me that the Jews of Yemen, including themselves, had been under this law for some thousands of years, that it gave them what they wanted, and that they would like to remain under it. I stipulated for two conditions, first, for evidence of the particular customs of the Yemen Jews, and secondly, for an assurance that any exemption granted to them should not be used as a precedent for granting a similar concession to the Jews of India generally. The stipulations were complied with by the production of evidence as to the laws and customs of Yemen Jews (very curious and interesting evidence it was), and by an undertaking from the leading Jews in British India that they would be content to remain under Anglo-Indian law. And the Jews of Aden were accordingly allowed to revert from Art. X. of 1865 to the Pentateuch."

Here we have an indication of the persistence with which a Semitic people adheres to its ancient customs, and we find in the matter of criminal law the same characteristic of unchangeableness. The Hebrew Law exhibits to us primitive usage of a similar type to that contained in the books of the Brehon Law; but the ideas of the two peoples were very different, and the contrast, as well as the comparison of the two systems, is most instructive.

The leading idea of the Hebrew Penal Law was the sanctity of human life. That man was created in the image of God was a precept of religion which was fully recognized by the Law. The life of a stranger was as much protected as that of one of the nation (*a*). To take it away involved the same sin and the

(*a*) Levit. xxiv. 22.

same offence. "That the life," says Ewald, "or, to express the idea in another more Hebrew word, the 'soul,' of a man possesses of itself an inviolable sanctity is one of the first principles which was firmly established among the nobler races from the very earliest times, and in which all those presentiments of something Infinite being implanted in man sought to find the clearest expression possible" (*a*).

The punishment for murder among the Hebrews, as among other primitive races, was *Revenge*. The relatives of the murdered man were allowed to retaliate. Vengeance of blood, as it was called, was always looked upon as a sacred duty with the nearest relatives of the deceased. To neglect to inflict it caused indelible disgrace. The Avenger of blood is the name invariably given to the next heir of the murdered man. Sometimes the whole family took the duty upon themselves, as in the story of the widow of Tekoah, told in the Book of Samuel:—"And, behold, the whole family is risen against thine handmaid, and they said, Deliver him that smote his brother, that we may kill him, for the life of his brother whom he slew" (2 Sam. xiv. 7). The punishment of death for homicide was invariable:—"He that smiteth a man, so that he die, shall surely be put to death" (Exod. xxi. 12). Retaliation was also enjoined or permitted for lesser offences. Life for life is only the application of the ordinary rule:—"If a man cause a blemish in his neighbour; as he hath done, so shall it be done to him; breach for breach, eye for eye, tooth for tooth: as he hath caused a blemish in a man, so shall it be rendered unto him" (Levit. xxiv. 19, 20). We are left in no doubt as to the manner of execution in case of murder:—"The manslayer shall surely be put to death. The avenger of blood shall himself put the manslayer to death: when he meeteth him he shall be put to death" (Numb. xxxv. 18). Here we have only another instance of the retaliation which is said by the *Senchus Mōr* to have existed in Ireland before the coming of Patrick.

(*a*) *Antiquities of Israel*, p. 168.

There is no trace of a judicial process of any kind, before the execution, in the Jewish Law. "*Whenever he meeteth* him he shall be put to death." There was no need even to justify the execution at any subsequent time before any assembly of any kind. Where death was caused the Avenger of blood was always justified in retaliating. Whether the murder was premeditated or not, the Avenger of blood had the same right of inflicting summary execution. Even in case of the accidental infliction of death, the unwilling slayer might be killed with impunity if he did not succeed in escaping to a city of refuge (Deut. xix. 6). And even though the slayer had so escaped to a city of refuge, and was there dwelling, if he left his place of refuge, even for the shortest possible time, he might be slain by the Avenger of blood, and the latter was guilty of no offence in slaying him (Numb. xxxv. 27, 28).

Such a system was not in any way peculiar to the Hebrews. It existed universally. The earliest mitigation among most communities of the terrible severity of this Law was the institution of the *death fine* as a substitute for the death penalty, at least in cases where the original slaying was accidental or unpremeditated. This death fine was at first a composition arranged between the Avenger of blood and the manslayer. I have already mentioned that it was almost universal in ancient law. It may possibly have existed among the Hebrews at an early stage of their history, but it is distinctly forbidden in the Mosaic legislation:—"Ye shall take no ransom for the life of a manslayer, which is guilty of death: but he shall surely be put to death" (Numb. xxxv. 31). "The acceptance of blood-money was not permitted in any form whatever, and so deep were the roots of this feeling that no special Hebrew word was found to express this mode of compensation" (*a*). (Ewald: *Antiquities of Israel*, p. 171.)

It was not only in the case of what we would call culpable homicide that the acceptance of a death fine was prohibited;

(*a*) The Hebrew word which is translated "ransom" in the English version, properly means *expiation*.

even in the case of accidental homicide commutation by a money payment was not permitted. A man who had escaped to a city of refuge, and was entitled to remain there, could not bargain with the Avenger of blood to be allowed to return to his home (Numb. xxxv. 32). In one exceptional case the acceptance of pecuniary compensation was permitted by the Law in lieu of the death penalty. When an ox, which was known by his owner to be dangerous, had gored a man, the owner was liable to be put to death; but "If there be laid on him a ransom, then he shall give for the redemption of his life whatsoever is laid upon him" (Exodus, xxi. 30). This was probably an exceptional permission of the continuance of a custom once more general. The very prohibition, in other cases, indicates the existence of the custom either among the people themselves or among surrounding tribes at some time or other.

No right of sanctuary was permitted for an intentional homicide. "If a man come presumptuously upon his neighbour, to slay him with guile; *thou shalt take him from mine altar*, that he may die" (Exodus, xxi. 14). But in the case of accidental homicide, the severity of the law was mitigated by the institution of the cities of refuge, where the person who so caused death might live in security. The fact that no place but one specially sacred was sufficient to protect even a man who had accidentally slain another, shows the terrible nature of the vengeance of blood which ancient Hebrew Law exacted.

It was only in cases where the death was caused entirely by accident that resort could be had to one of the cities of refuge. "This is the case of the manslayer, which shall flee thither and live; whoso killeth his neighbour unawares, and hated him not in time past; as when a man goeth into the forest with his neighbour to hew wood, and his hand fetcheth a stroke with the axe to cut down the tree, and the head slippeth from the helve, and lighteth upon his neighbour, that he die; he shall flee unto one of these cities, and live; lest the avenger of blood pursue the manslayer, while his heart is hot, and overtake him, because the way is long, and smite him mortally;

whereas he was not worthy of death, inasmuch as he hated him not in time past" (Deut. xix. 4–6).

Although the original institution of the cities of refuge was for cases of pure accident only, it is probable that where death was caused in a sudden attack, or in the heat of a quarrel, without *malice*, as we would say in our law, a resort to a city of refuge was allowed. This would appear to be the natural meaning of one passage in the Book of Numbers (xxxv. 22, 23). But apparently if a stone or a deadly weapon was used, such excuse could not be pleaded; and although there might have been no intention to cause death, the offender was given over to vengeance.

The primitive retaliation among the Hebrews was, as elsewhere, entirely a custom, without any judicial process or condemnation. It is in connexion with the right of sanctuary in a city of refuge that we find the first trace in Hebrew Law of a judicial investigation. The right of refuge only existed, as I have said, in the case of accidental homicide; it was therefore necessary to decide, in any case where it was claimed, whether the person who claimed it was entitled to the privilege. Upon arriving at the city of refuge, the fugitive was bound to stand at the entrance-gate and "declare his cause in the ears of the elders of that city" (Joshua, xx. 4). If he made a *prima facie* case he was admitted, and once admitted could not be surrendered to the Avenger of blood. But suppose the slayer had really committed murder, and procured admission to the city of refuge by a false account of the transaction, what was done? Once the right of refuge was allowed, subject to certain restrictions, it was necessary to determine judicially in what cases it might be availed of. This was done, not as we might expect, by the authorities of the city of refuge, but by the elders of the city from which the manslayer had fled. It was their duty upon complaint made by the Avenger of blood to send to the city of refuge for the accused, and there to determine the matter whether the slaying was accidental or not. If it was, they restored the accused to his city of refuge, where, notwithstanding his acquittal of any intention to do wrong, he was bound to remain until the death of the High Priest; if, on the other hand, they decided that the slaying was not excusable, they delivered the culprit over to the Avenger of blood for vengeance. This appears quite clearly from a comparison of two passages, one in the Book of Numbers, and the other in the Book of Deuteronomy:—"If any man hate his neighbour, and lie in wait for him, and rise up against him, and smite him mortally that he die; and he flee into one of these cities: then *the elders of his city shall send and fetch him thence*, and deliver him into the hand of the avenger of blood" (Deut. xix. 11, 12). From this account alone we might suppose that the trial took place in the absence of the accused, before he was sent for, and that it was only in case of his conviction that he was brought back to his own city. The passage in the Book of Numbers, however, shows that this was not so. It appears from it that the accused was brought back for trial in every case. After enumerating the various cases of excusable homicide, it goes on:—"Then the congregation shall judge between the smiter and the avenger of blood according to these judgments: and the congregation shall deliver the manslayer out of the hand of the avenger of blood, *and the congregation shall restore him to his city of refuge, whither he was fled;* and he shall dwell therein until the death of the high priest, which was anointed with the holy oil" (Numb. xxxv. 24, 25). It is plain from this account that the judicial inquiry by the elders of the city was confined to cases where the accused had fled to a city of refuge, and had been brought back thence. The congregation is merely to *restore* the accused to the city of refuge, *whither he was fled.* If the avenger of blood were able to kill him, before he first reached the city of refuge, it was lawful for him to do so with impunity.

It was necessary that two witnesses should testify to his guilt, before the refugee was given over for execution. "One witness shall not testify against any person that he die" (Numb. xxxv. 30), *i. e.* apparently some person should corroborate the accuser, if the accused pleaded that the deed was accidental. Naturally everyone who caused the death of another would flee to a city of refuge as his only chance of escape, and in nearly every case he would be demanded by the avenger of blood. The investigation by the elders of the city would thus come to be a universal custom in cases of homicide (except in cases where the avenger of blood had actually slain the culprit before he reached the city of refuge). In this manner the transition from the primitive system of revenge to a regular criminal trial is complete, the only trace of the former system being the execution of the sentence by the avenger of blood personally.

The Hebrew Law thus, by the prohibition of the death fine, and the institution of cities for refuge, as a mitigation of the primitive custom of revenge, developed itself in an entirely different manner from the Law amongst Aryan communities. With the latter the first origin of a judicial trial is the reference to arbitration of the amount of the death fine to be paid. There is no reference to arbitration, and no trace of its existence, so far as I am aware, in the Hebrew Law. The jurisdiction of the elders to determine a question as to the accidental character of the deed or otherwise is of an entirely different nature, and was probably the real origin of Criminal Law.

Bodily injuries not causing death were subject to the rule of retaliation also. The Lex Talionis was applied here as rigorously as in the case of death. "If a man cause a blemish in his neighbour; as he hath done, so shall it be done to him; breach for breach, eye for eye, tooth for tooth" (Levit. xxiv. 19–20). It is probable that this rule was confined to the case of intentional injuries. "That unintentional injuries," says Ewald, "would not be intended here is a matter of course. Even in the case of those that were intentional, the law interfered only at the express suit of the injured person; and undoubtedly in later times compensation for injuries was mostly made in money" (*a*).

(*a*) *Antiquities of Israel*, p. 175.

There was no prohibition of the acceptance of compensation in this case. If a man, for instance, hurt a woman with child, so as to produce a premature delivery, but no further harm happened to her, it was provided that the offender in this case should be fined, "according as the woman's husband shall lay upon him, and he shall pay as the judges determine" (Ex. xxi. 22). If, however, mischief followed to the woman, "then," said the Law, "thou shalt give life for life" (*ibid.* ver. 23).

Bodily hurt in a quarrel could also be compensated for, the Law providing that the offender "shall pay for the loss of his time, and shall cause him to be thoroughly healed" (*ibid.* ver. 19). This was apparently where both were equally in fault originally. But in the case of intentional injuries, the *lex talionis* was enforced with all its rigour, and although there was no prohibition against a money composition, there was no obligation on the injured person to accept same. "Life shall go for life, eye for eye, tooth for tooth, hand for hand, foot for foot" (Deut. xix. 21).

So far was this principle carried that it was applied even in the case of false testimony. The offence of false testimony necessarily involves the existence of a judicial inquiry, and so belongs to a later stage of civilization than that which sanctions revenge. Still the principle is maintained. A similar punishment is inflicted to that which the victim would himself naturally wish to impose. It is provided in the Book of Deuteronomy (xix. 16–20) that "If an unrighteous witness rise up against any man to testify against him of wrong-doing, then both the men, between whom the controversy is, shall stand before the Lord before the Priests and the Judges, which shall be in those days; and the Judges shall make diligent inquisition; and behold, if the witness be a false witness, and hath testified falsely against his brother, *then shall ye do unto him, as he hath thought to do unto his brother.*"

Private property, both in moveables and in land, was recognized by the Hebrew Law. Instances of land being allotted to deserving chiefs and soldiers are frequent in the Old Testament. Hebron, for instance, was given to Caleb by Joshua, immediately after the conquest (Josh. xiv. 6–15). Upon death, property was divided amongst the sons, the first-born being entitled to a double portion (Deut. xxi. 15–17. "The first-born was the principal heir and the proper representative of the family, but undoubtedly under the condition of taking upon himself more of the duties of the head of the family than the other brothers, of maintaining the widows, and of providing for the unmarried daughters" (Ewald, *Antiquities of Israel*, p. 179). Daughters inherited fixed property only under exceptional circumstances, with the consent of their father or their brothers. But if there were no sons, the daughters took the property in equal shares (Numb. xxvii. 8). This was the "rule in Zelophehad's case," referred to by Mr. Ilbert, which is still observed by the Jews of Aden.

Laws for the protection of property were unusually strict: Ex. xxii. 1–4. A thief detected during the nihgt might be slain with impunity; if he were caught in the daytime he could not be slain, but he was bound to make restitution twofold or fourfold according as he had disposed of the property or not. If he had nothing, and was therefore unable to pay the necessary sum, he was sold into slavery for his debt.

Here we notice a striking similarity to the early Roman Law. The same privilege of killing a nocturnal thief caught in the act is conferred upon the owner of the stolen goods; the punishment, a money penalty only, in other cases varying, not according to moral guilt, but according to the time of detection and the value of the article stolen. There was also the same liability of a convicted thief to be sold into slavery if he were unable to pay the debt. Primitive penal law appears to have been much the same everywhere.

Theft of human beings was punished by death (Deut. xxiv. 7), whether the stolen person was found in possession of the thief, or had been sold by him into slavery (Ex. xxi. 16). This severity of the law was necessary, owing to the continual growth of the slave trade, especially in latter times.

The paternal rights over children, recognized by the customs of all early nations, are found also in the Hebrew Law; and apparently a father was allowed, for the most trifling offence, to take the life of his children (Deut. xxi. 18–21). But this *jus vitae necisque* was not by any means so arbitrary as that which the ancient Roman Law allowed. The Book of Deuteronomy distinctly lays it down that parents were not themselves to inflict the penalty, but that they were to bring the matter before the whole community, who were to inflict the punishment. This may have been, and probably was, a restriction on the primitive absolute right of life and death vested in the father. The punishment for adultery and unnatural offences was likewise stoning by the community (Deut. xxii. 21).

We thus see that among the most important of Semitic peoples, the general course of development of Penal Law was the same as among Aryan communities. The instinct of Revenge is the origin of the Law. Regulations as to the manner of its exercise gradually arise; and in some exceptional cases, the punishment is taken in hand by the public authorities, in order to prevent an excessive or unjust exercise of the privilege. The principle of retaliation continues, however, to be the sole principle upon which the Law is based.

II.—MOHAMMEDAN LAW.

The Mohammedan Law exhibits, as we might naturally expect, the same traces of primitive usage in relation to crimes and offences. Nothing is more opposed to the spirit of Islam than the idea of progress; and even until the present day, in countries ruled by Mohammedan Law, the same principles and practices prevail as were in existence more than a thousand years ago. The Penal Code adopted in the Turkish Empire in 1840 introduced more modern ideas; and the Koran has, in many respects, been tacitly abandoned. The latter is, however, still recognized as the principal, if not the sole, authority in legal matters. The identification of law with religion, here also, opposed an almost insuperable obstacle to legal development. The only loophole for escape, for legal ideas, from the narrow prison of the Koran, lay in the principle of tradition. Pious Mussulmans, while acknowledging the absolute authority of the Koran in legal matters, do not assert that it has left nothing unsaid, or that a precept for every case must be found in it. They hold, on the contrary, that many things were revealed to Mohammed which were not written down by him, but which were orally communicated to his companions, who have carefully transmitted them to future generations of the faithful. According to an Arab author of high repute, *El Magrizi*, the decisions of the Prophet upon special cases which called for his intervention were known often only to humble followers who were with him at the time, and escaped the notice of others. Thus, in one case where Omar was ignorant as to what was the proper fine (*Dia*) due for an unborn infant, a humble Arab of Hodaïl was able to tell the Prophet's decision in a similar case (*a*).

Tradition is always more or less elastic, and in all probability traditions, conveniently invented, assisted much in the growth of the law in various branches. It is not, therefore, surprising to find considerable diversity of detail arising in different systems of Mussulman Law.

The Mohammedan Penal Law is based upon the same principle of primitive retaliation and self-redress as the other systems to which I have referred. We have the same absence of State intervention, and the same custom of death fines as we find to have existed under the Brehon Laws. "Dans les sociétés," says M. Albert Du Boys (*b*), "où l'on n'a fait, en quelque sorte, que régulariser l'exercice du droit de vengeance, où le talion existe dans sa grossièreté native, l'état n' intervient que pour sanctionner ce talion, ou pour le remplacer par une

(*a*) See *Etudes sur la Loi Musulmane*, par C. Vincent, p. 15.
(*b*) *Histoire du Droit Criminal des Peuples Modernes*, vol. i., p. 366.

composition pécuniaire par laquelle il règle les conditions mises à la rançon du meurtrier et au pardon des parents de la victime."

The Koran lays down in the most absolute terms this principle of retaliation in the case of murder, and at the same time it also expressly allows the relatives of the slain to take a ransom (called *Dia*, or price of blood) for his life. "O true believers, the law of retaliation is ordained you for the slain: the free shall die for the free, and the servant for the servant, &c., woman for a woman, but he whom his brother shall forgive may be prosecuted and obliged to make satisfaction, according to what is just, and a fine shall be set on him with humanity" (Koran, chap. ii.). "Whosoever shall be slain unjustly we have given his heir power to demand satisfaction; but let him not exceed the bounds of moderation in putting to death the murderer in too cruel a manner, or by revenging his friend's blood on any other than the person who killed him; since he is assisted by this law" (*ibid.* chap. xvii.)

This is the common practice in Mohammedan countries, such as Persia, to the present day. The relatives of the deceased have their choice either to have the murderer put into their hands to be put to death, or else to accept a pecuniary satisfaction (*a*). In Turkey, until a very recent time, murder was never prosecuted by the public authorities. The nearest relations were allowed to revenge the slaughter of their kinsman if they thought fit; or if they preferred (as they generally did) to accept the *Dia*, or price of blood, they could do so, and the murderer then escaped liability. The Penal Code of 1840, however, entirely abolished this system of pecuniary compensation, and imposed the penalty of death for murder in every case (Art. 10). The *Code Moulteka* had, in 1824, in a great measure effected this end; but the right to the payment of the *Dia* was preserved by it in some exceptional cases.

In the case of accidental killing, a fine was also payable to

(*a*) See Chardin, *Voyage de Perse*, vol. ii., p. 299. Sale, Translation of the Koran, p. 19 (note).

the family of deceased, if they were true believers. "Whoso killeth a believer by mistake, the penalty shall be the freeing of a believer from slavery, and a fine to be paid to the family of the deceased, unless they remit it as alms" (Koran, chap. iv.); but if the offender was unable to pay the fine, vengeance was not to be exacted. He was obliged to fast two months consecutively, and so became free. The fine was in all cases divisible among the relatives of the deceased according to the laws of inheritance laid down in the Koran itself.

Theft was originally punished by mutilation. The hand, as the offending member, was first cut off as a suitable retaliation. For a second offence the thief lost his foot, and so on, until all his members were amputated. But, as in the case of homicide, the owners of the stolen property might compound with the thief, and accept whatever penalty in lieu of revenge they thought right. "Composition," it is laid down in a work of authority (*a*), "is lawful with respect to every right or claim for which a consideration may legally be taken, whether the right or thing compromised be capable of being sold (as actual property), or incapable (like the compensation for a crime or offence, or for wilful bloodshed, the right of occupancy of a house, and the compensation for a defect or blemish in an article bought). Further, in the case of a compromise of the right of retaliation, whether it be executed for more, or less, than the *decŭt*, or fine of blood, it is equally legal and valid; but in the case of accidental homicide, if it be executed for more than the *decŭt*, or fine fixed by the law, and that be of the same species, and of a nature in which usury can take place, the validity of the composition is liable to doubt."

The Penal Code of 1840 abolished mutilation for theft, throughout the Turkish Empire, and substituted therefor a maximum term of seven years' imprisonment as a penalty. Previous to the adoption of this Code there was really no such thing as Criminal Law existing in Turkey. The primitive

(*a*) Digest of Mohammedan Law according to the Sect of the Twelve Imams, p. 385.

right of personal revenge which existed in lieu thereof, being capable of being compounded for on exactly the same principles as a right of property of any kind. The law was in almost every respect identical with that existing in Ireland under the Brehon system. Identity of usage could not have arisen from any intercourse between the Celtic tribes of Ireland and the Semitic races of Asia. The similarity of custom arose rather from the simple fact that human nature is very much the same everywhere, and that, consequently, the course of development of Penal Law is extremely like in the most distant countries.

LECTURE IV.

THE ROMAN PENAL LAW.

IN studying the Roman system of Laws the importance of the distinction between *Criminal* Law and *Penal* Law becomes extremely marked. The notion of a crime was of exceedingly slow development in Rome. The theory of *punishment* by means of a civil action was well recognized in the matured Roman system. Real Criminal Law did not appear at Rome until a much later stage of legal history than it did in England. While the Republic was in its prime there was practically none in existence. It was only when it began to waste away that we find true Criminal Law coming into existence. The *Leges Corneliæ* passed by Sulla about the year 81 B.C. were the earliest statutes which punished offences against individuals as public wrongs. From this time forward numerous statutes were passed dealing with particular offences, until under the Empire the general rule was adopted that anyone who could bring a penal action on a delict might, if he preferred it, prosecute the delinquent before a criminal tribunal. (*a*)

The slow development of the Criminal Law is extremely remarkable, in contrast to the very rapid manner in which the Civil Law developed itself. The earliest view we get of the Roman Civil Law exhibits it, in a great measure, already

(*a*) *See* Mr. Moyle's note to *Just. Inst.* book iv., tit. 2, and D. 47. 1. 3, and D. 47. 2. 56. 1.

free from the formalism and superstition which usually pervade early systems of law.

"The chief result," says the historian Mommsen, of an inquiry into the ancient jurisprudence of the people of Italy, "may be summed up in saying that fewer traces, comparatively, of the primitive state of things have been preserved in the case of the Italians, and the Romans in particular, than in the case of any other Indo-Germanic race. The bow and arrow, the war-chariot, the incapacity of women to hold property, the acquiring of wives by purchase, the primitive form of burial, human sacrifices, blood revenge, the clan constitution conflicting with the authority of the community, a lively natural symbolism: all these, and numerous phenomena of a kindred character, must be presumed to have lain at the foundation of civilization in Italy as well as elsewhere; but at the epoch when that civilization comes clearly into view they have wholly disappeared, and it is only the comparison of kindred races which informs us that such things once existed. In this respect Italian history begins at a far later stage of civilization than *e. g.* the Greek or the Germanic, and from the first it exhibits a comparatively modern character." (*a*)

Sir. H. Maine fixes the origin of true Criminal Law in Rome at the year 149 B.C., when the Lex Calpurnia de Repetundis was passed. (*b*) This statute established the first Quæstio Perpetua or permanent criminal tribunal, and thus from the point of view of criminal procedure it may be considered the origin of the Criminal Law; and as its object was to punish the misappropriation of public funds by Provincial Governors, it dealt with what is undoubtedly a crime, but it does not clearly recognize what is the gist of Criminal Law,—that an injury to an individual may be a public wrong. It dealt only with a direct injury to the State, although individuals might of course be indirectly injured thereby. The *Leges Corneliæ*, however, passed some 70 years later, dealt with murder, arson, forgery, and such matters, where the offence

(*a*) *Hist. of Rome,* vol. i. p. 157. (*b*) *Ancient Law,* Chap. x. p. 384.

was directly against the individual, and the State was only wronged in so far as alarm was created or public order disturbed. From this legislation therefore we may date the origin of true Criminal Law at Rome. It never really obtained any great importance, and such offences as theft (*furtum*) and robbery (*vi bonorum raptorum*) were always dealt with as delicts rather than as crimes in the Roman Law.

In the English legal system, on the other hand, the notion of a crime was very early developed, and the Criminal Law always occupied a prominent place. The penal actions, on the other hand, which occupy such an important position in the Roman system, gradually disappeared, or became merged in ordinary actions of tort. The difference between the two systems arose probably from the different form of government, and is one of the many illustrations of the necessity for the historical study of law. The Roman form of government being a Republic, the English a Monarchy, the notion of an injury to the State through an injury to an individual was much more easy to comprehend in the latter case than in the former. The State was an impersonal abstraction at Rome. In England it was represented by a distinct individual, who would naturally punish as a wrong to himself an injury committed against anyone under his protection. When we come to consider the development of the English Criminal Law we shall see what an important part the personal position of the King took in it; the violation of the King's peace being at first the fact, and afterwards the fiction, upon which every criminal charge was grounded.

The Roman Law is interesting as being the only important system of laws which has grown up under a republic, and it affords us also the best example of a logically developed system of private penal jurisprudence. It is also interesting on account of another peculiarity in contrast to most other systems, viz. its freedom from religious influence. The distinction between a *sin* and a *crime*, as Professor Hunter remarks, "lies at the root of all legal development;" but it is not, in general, recognized until a comparatively late period. Indeed, even at the present day, the notion of punishing sins *as sins* is not entirely extinct in our Criminal Law, while the early English Law fully recognized the principle of doing so. The Romans were not a religious people, and they adopted the sensible principle of allowing the gods to avenge their own injuries. Thus, in the later law, the distinction between perjury as an offence against the gods, and false testimony as an offence against man was well recognized. Perjury as such was not a crime unless the accused swore *per genium Principis*, in which case he was considered to have offered an insult to the Emperor. Laws against heresy, when enacted, were justified upon the grounds that new forms of worship tended to disturb the minds of weak persons (*a*).

The non-religious character of Roman Law was another cause, probably, of the slow development of the Criminal Law. Amongst a religious people, the idea that it is a public duty to punish a sin is more likely to arise than that a private wrong should be so avenged ; and it is extremely likely that in many cases private injuries, such as murder and theft, were punished in the first instance by the State as sins rather than as torts. The callousness of the Romans as regards the punishment of sins against the gods probably contributed, with other causes, to the slow development of Criminal Law, and the importance of private Penal Law.

The earliest known Laws of the Roman people are comprised in the code called the XII. Tables, which was compiled by the Decemvirs about the year 450 B.C. An ancient code differs essentially from a modern code in this, that the latter, unlike the former, is supposed to be a piece of new legislation entirely superseding the laws previously prevailing. Such a compilation as the XII. Tables, however, was considered only as a summary of the existing law, for the purpose of informing those who were bound to obey, what rules they were obliged to follow. We can thus rely upon finding in such a code, traces at least of the

(*a*) Paul. Sent., 5. 21–2.

Primitive Law of the people. Unfortunately the greater portion of the XII. Tables is now lost. Fragments are, however, preserved through the frequent references to the code in the writings of the classical jurists. Gaius constantly refers to it; and from these scattered references modern scholars have attempted to reconstruct the Tables. A complete collection of the existing fragments, with references to the passages in later writings, stating the purport of others now lost, may be found in Ortolan's *Histoire de la Legislation Romaine.*

We find in the XII. Tables, as we might naturally expect, that there is no trace of Criminal Law in our modern signification of the term :—no punishment inflicted by the State for an injury done to an individual. Self-redress is the principle recognized here as in all Ancient Law. Table VIII. deals with delicts, and is the source of the later Roman Law of torts and crimes. There is no extant provision as regards homicide. It is stated by Pliny (*Hist. Nat.* xviii. 3.) that the punishment for this offence was death, but we have no knowledge of how this punishment was inflicted. It can scarcely have been by a regular judicial sentence, or we should have some record of a change in the law in this respect; for capital punishment was not practised in historical times at Rome. The probability is that the infliction of death was here as elsewhere merely *sanctioned* by the Law, if inflicted, in retaliation, by the near relatives of the murdered man. Such was apparently the rule with regard to serious bodily injuries not causing death. The words of Table VIII. with reference to such injuries are "Si membrum rupit, ni cum eo pacit, talio esto." "If a person break another's limb, *unless he comes to terms with him*, let there be retaliation." This passage affords us a good illustration of the point of view in which Ancient Law regarded torts and crimes. Modern Law both *punishes* the wrongdoer and *compensates* the injured person for a wrongful act, such as an assault. The act in reference to the punishment is called a crime, in reference to the compensation a tort. Ancient Law recognized no such distinction. It simply allowed the injured man or his relations to punish the wrongdoer unless the latter was able to buy off vengeance by a money payment. The *Talio* was inflicted by the nearest relative (*a*). The XII. Tables thus bring us in this provision to the very threshold of Penal Law:—simple retaliation—" *Talio esto.*" The custom of retaliation is recognized as reasonable. The custom of the wrongdoer buying off the revenge is also recognized and encouraged by the Law, but in no way enjoined. The tendency of the Law was, as I have said, to encourage these pecuniary compositions, with a view to preventing disorder. The XII. Tables, in the case of lesser injuries, fix the amount of the compensation to be paid absolutely. Thus according to Table VIII.:—"Si injuriam faxit, alteri viginti quinque aeris pœnae sunto." "Injuria" apparently is here used to signify slight assaults, libels, &c. "Injuria" says Gaius, "is inflicted not only when anyone strikes another with his fist, or with a stick, or whip, but also by using abusive language (*convicium*), or when anyone wrongfully seizes the goods of another, knowing that he owes him nothing, and advertises them for sale, or by writing defamatory statements or songs, or by following about a matron or a young boy, or in many other ways" (Gaius, iii. 220).

A law which provided a fixed penalty for all cases of assault, slander, libel, illegal seizure, and solicitation, seems strange to us; and it is probable that this sum of 25 asses was only a suggested amount of what would be reasonable in ordinary cases as between the parties. We know from Gaius that in his time, at any rate, there was no fixed sum, but that the Praetor or the Judex, according to the nature of the injury, fixed the amount of the penalty (Gaius, iii. 224). In the case of damage caused accidentally the rule was simply that it should be repaired.

The theory of the Ancient Penal Law being thus revenge, the amount of the punishment awarded, or of the damages or penalty assessed, varied, not according to the moral guilt of the

(*a*) Talione proximus cognatus ulciscitur.—Cato, in Priscian, 6. 700.

delinquent, nor according to the injury sustained by the injured party, but rather in proportion to the provocation. The Law sanctioned what would be a natural amount of punishment, and provided as a measure of damages what an injured person would be likely to accept as the price of surrendering his alternative right of revenge. This theory pervaded the whole Roman Law of delicts or torts, even in its most mature stage.

In addition to the provisions regarding personal injuries, the extant fragments of Table VIII. contain provisions as to theft, fraud by a patron on his client, incantations, administration of poisons, and the curious offence of a witness to the solemn form of contract by nexum refusing afterwards to testify as to the transaction. The punishment provided for this offence was based upon the same principle of retaliation, which was applied in other cases. The person offending became infamous. He was incapable of giving evidence himself for the future, and no person was allowed to give evidence in his favour.

During the whole period of the Republic at Rome, Criminal Law can scarcely be said to have existed. Crimes were punished by penal actions, *i. e.* actions which conferred upon the person injured a right to recover a penalty as a *punishment* to the wrongdoer, not as a means of providing *compensation* to the sufferer. It is not correct, however, to speak of these *actions ex delicto* as corresponding to our actions of tort, for our law of torts is almost entirely based upon the principle of compensation rather than punishment. They were rather a substitute for our modern criminal prosecutions.

Obligations *ex delicto* always involved either *dolus* or *culpa.* "Dolus" is a term constantly occurring in the Roman Law, and is generally translated by the English term "fraud." In reference to contracts this rendering is fairly accurate, but when used in reference to delicts it has a somewhat different signification. It means a general unlawful intention—a deliberate intention to violate the law. "Dolus" is thus very nearly equivalent to our term "Malice." "Malice," in law, does not denote anything with reference to the motive by which a man is actuated. It implies only that he has a deliberate intention to do a wrongful act. "Malice" is really equivalent to "criminal intention." "Culpa" is exactly equivalent to "negligence." The rule, therefore, that a person only incurred an *obligatio ex delicto* when he acted either with *dolus* or *culpa* exactly corresponds to the English rule as to criminal liability, that a person can only be held liable for a criminal offence, if he has acted either with "malice"—*i. e.* a deliberate intention to break the law—or with such gross "negligence," as the law considers to be equivalent to intention.

The remedy for a delict in Roman Law was invariably a *penal action.* The penalty was in some cases fixed by law; in others it was based on the value of the property taken or injured; and in others, as in the case of *Injuriæ* in the time of Gaius, it was assessed either by the Praetor or the Judex. In the case of an action which was purely penal, such as the action of theft, the right to recover the penalty was entirely separate and distinct from the right to recover the article stolen. In other cases what was called a "mixed action" was allowed, namely, one in which both the penalty and compensation for the injury could be recovered (Just. Inst., 4, 6, 18). Of this class of action were those for robbery (*vi bonorum raptorum*) and *Damnum Injuriæ* under the *Lex Aquilia.* These actions appear to have been later in origin than the action of theft, which always remained the most archaic of all actions *ex delicto.* The *actio furti* did not, as is sometimes said, correspond to our action of trover. Its sole object was to recover the penalty and the property itself; or its value was recoverable in another form of action, corresponding to our action of trover. "*Pœnam tantum persequitur quis actione furti:* sive enim manifesti agatur quadrupli sive nec manifesti dupli, de sola pœna agitur: *nam ipsam rem propria actione* persequitur quis, id est suam esse petens, sive fur ipse eam rem possideat, sive alius quilibet: eo amplius adversus furem etiam condictio est rei" (Just. Inst. 4, 6, 18).

And it is also laid down in the *Digest* that if a person hires a slave and then appropriates him, the two actions, one for the breach of contract and the other for the theft, may be maintained. "Si locatum tibi servum subripies, utrumque judicium adversus te est exercendum, locati et furti" (*D.* 19. 2. 42). In the same way in our own law, an owner of property stolen can prosecute for theft and at the same time bring a civil action in trover to recover the value of the goods stolen; but he cannot commence the action, one in contract and one in tort, arising out of exactly the same state of facts, for the law forbids what is called the splitting of the cause of action.

Penal actions, being based on the theory of punishment, were naturally not available against the heir of the wrongdoer. "Est enim certissima juris regula ex malificiis pœnales actiones in heredem non competere, veluti furti, vi bonorum raptorum, injuriarum, damni injuriæ" (J. 4, 12, 1). Thus also in our own Criminal Law, the death of the accused puts an end to a prosecution; but the principle of the Roman Law in this respect has been also applied in our Common Law, with a complete ignorance of its origin and limitation, the maxim "actio *pœnalis* moritur cum persona" being transferred into "actio *personalis* moritur cum persona." No legal maxim has caused so much confusion in our law as this. It is impossible to hand down any general rule as to when it applies and when it does not. The confusion and uncertainty thus produced should be a solemn warning against the adoption of principles from other legal systems without a complete understanding of their origin and real limits.

The measure of damages in the Roman Law in the case of obligations *ex contractu*, and obligations *quasi ex delicto*, properly so called, was very much the same as that in our own law in the case of actions of contract—namely, the amount by which the property of the injured party would have been greater if the obligation had been fulfilled or the harmful act or event had not occurred "id quod interest," "quanti ea res est." A *pretium affectionis* which was purely personal and not pecuniary was not taken into account. The theory of compensation was applied strictly and regularly. In the case of obligations *ex delicto* the principle applied was not compensation, but punishment or vindication. The measure of damages was not "id quod interest," or what loss the Plaintiff had sustained, but rather what would be a fit and suitable punishment for the offence; and this, in the first instance at all events, was based on a calculation of what the injured party would be content to take in consideration of his foregoing his right to revenge.

The main distinction between obligations *ex delicto* and obligations *quasi ex delicto* was this, that the former implied some moral guilt, something deserving of punishment; the latter, as a general rule, arose out of facts which did not imply any moral delinquency, but only a certain amount of negligence, sufficient in the view of the law to put the loss upon the person who had been guilty of the negligence rather than upon the sufferer thereby. The principal cases in which obligations *quasi ex delicto* arose were those where persons were held responsible for the fault of others, such as masters for the acts of their servants (*a*); but although the greater part of such obligations arose in this way vicariously, still all did not. A Judex who gives a wrong decision (si judex litem suam fecerit) was considered liable *quasi ex delicto*. He was liable, even though he had erred through ignorance (*per imprudentiam*). If he acted corruptly, there was of course *dolus*, and in such cases what we would call exemplary damages could be recovered (Just. 4, 5, par). The distinction in principle between liability *ex delicto* and *quasi ex delicto* was not strictly adhered to, though it existed. The Roman Law, like our own Law, was in many cases badly classified, but a distinction nevertheless existed. In our own law of torts no such distinction is recognized, and consequently very great confusion and uncertainty exists as to the measure of damages. The *theory* in all cases in English Law is compensation, but in a considerable number of torts, principles are applied quite inconsistent with this theory; and we may fairly say that all cases where juries are allowed to award exemplary

(*a*) As to the origin of the liability in such cases see *ante*, pp. 5 and 6.

damages are cases where the principle applied is punishment, not compensation. These cases of actions ought to be classed by themselves, and carefully distinguished from cases where only compensation is awarded; but this has never been done. The result of the non-recognition of this distinction has been to introduce confusion and uncertainty into the rules of English Law on the measure of damages in actions of tort.

Delicts in the mature system of Roman Jurisprudence were divided into four classes—(1) Theft (*furtum*); (2) Robbery (*vi bonorum raptorum*); (3) Injuries to property (*Damnum injuriæ per legem Aquiliam*); and (4) Injuries to the person (*Injuriæ*). Theft and Injuries to the person (*Injuriæ*) are mentioned in the XII. Tables. Robbery was not originally distinguished from theft. Cicero tells us that it was constituted a separate delict by the edict of the Praetor Lucullus in the year 77, B. C. Damnum Injuriæ was also constituted a specific delict by the *Lex Aquilia* about the year 285 B. C. It was never the subject of criminal prosecution, as the other three were. *Furta* and *Injuriæ* thus represent in Primitive Penal Law at Rome the two great classes of offences which exist in every system of Penal Law—(1) Injuries to property; and (2) Injuries to the person. As they are mentioned in the earliest records of the Roman Law and were gradually developed with its growth much in the same way as their analogies in English Law, their history is both interesting and instructive.

There were originally in the Roman Law four distinct actions of theft, namely—(1) Theft detected in the commission (*furtum manifestum*); (2) Theft not so detected (*furtum nec manifestum*); (3) Possession of stolen property discovered upon search (*furtum conceptum*); and (4) The introduction of stolen property (*furtum oblatum*) (*a*).

"The penalty" (*pœna*), says Gaius (*b*), "by the law of the Twelve Tables, was capital for *furtum manifestum.* A free man was scourged and delivered over to the person from whom he had stolen (whether he became a slave by the delivery or

(*a*) Gaius, *Inst.*, 3, 183. (*b*) *Inst.* 3, 189.

reduced to the condition of an insolvent judgment debtor was an old question). A slave was first scourged and then flung from the Tarpeian rock. Afterwards the severity of this penalty was disapproved, and by the edict of the Praetor an action for fourfold damages was constituted in the case both of theft by a slave and by a free man.

"The penalty for *furtam nec manifestum* by the law of the Twelve Tables was double damages: this the Praetor has preserved.

"The penalty for *furtum conceptum* and *furtum oblatum* by the law of the Twelve Tables was triple damages: this has been retained by the Praetor."

This passage has been frequently cited to illustrate the entirely different view taken by ancient and modern law of wrongful acts. Without an historical knowledge of the fact we could never have conceived that the distinction between different forms of an offence should depend altogether upon the time and manner in which it was detected. The modern ideas of punishment for the sake of reforming the criminal, and preventing a repetition of the offence, have no place in Primitive Law. Vengeance against the wrongdoer is the sole object which is aimed at.

"The reason," says Mr. Poste, "why *furtum manifestum* was subjected to a heavier penalty than *furtum nec manifestum* was not because the barbarous legislator supposed that detection in the act was an aggravation of the offence, but because he wished, by the amplitude of the legal remedy offered, to induce the aggrieved party not to take the law into his own hands and inflict summary vengeance on the offender, particularly as it was lawful to kill a nocturnal thief, or one who during the day defended himself with a weapon. In the infancy of society it is an important object to the legislator to induce an injured person to have recourse to the public tribunals instead of righting himself, that is to say, constituting himself both lawgiver and judge (*a*)."

(*a*) Poste's *Gaius*, p. 460.

It would perhaps be more true to say that the Ancient Lawgiver sanctioned the recovery of such a penalty as the person wronged would probably be content to take. The notion of tribunals being set up and persons being induced to enter them, as it were by a bribe, is entirely contrary to fact. Law existed before lawgivers or legal tribunals; and tribunals when they grew into existence simply ascertained what was the prevailing custom for settling the particular class of cases with which they dealt. "The standard of punishment," as Mr. Hunter says, "was thus determined with a regard to the feelings of vengeance that might be expected to actuate a sufferer taking into his own hands the punishment for the depredations on his property."

There is a striking analogy in the early English Laws to this variation of the punishment, depending upon the time of apprehension rather than upon the character of the offence, not, indeed, in the case of theft, but in reference to the offence which has become the foundation of the whole Criminal Law of England—breach of the King's peace. The Law of King Alfred imposed death as the penalty for fighting in the King's hall if the offender was taken in the act. If he escaped and was subsequently apprehended, "wer-gild" only was exacted. "If any one fight in the King's hall, or draw his weapon, and he be taken, be it in the King's doom either death or life, as he may be willing to grant him. If he escape and be taken again, let him pay for himself according to his 'wer-gild,' and make 'bōt' for the offence, as well 'wēr' as 'wite,' according as he may have wrought" (*a*).

The various differences which existed between the Roman and English Law of theft arose chiefly from the different definitions adopted in each system (*b*). Thus the term *contrectatio*, although it implied some overt act—" neque verbo, neque

(*a*) Thorpe, *Ancient Laws and Institutes of England*, p. 30.

(*b*) For a definition of theft, according to Roman Law, see *Digest*, 47, 2, 1, 3, and according to English Law, the judgment of BOVILL, C. J., in Reg. *v.* Middleton, L. R. 2 C. C. R. at p. 46.

scriptura quis furtum facit" (*D.* 47. 2. 52. 19)—yet it did not require that the offence should be complete at the actual moment when possession was first taken by the thief. According to English Law, if the first "taking" is lawful, no subsequent fraudulent dealing amounts to theft. Thus, supposing a man's house takes fire, and his neighbour takes his goods with his consent for the purpose of protecting them, if the neighbour afterwards changes his mind and converts them to his own use, this is not larceny in English Law, as the original "taking" was lawful (*a*), but in Roman Law it would clearly be theft, the subsequent appropriation being a sufficient "*contrectatio.*"

In spite of these points of difference, the Roman Law of theft was in the main the same as our own. Thus, in the important case of the finding of lost property, the Romans applied exactly the same test as to whether the appropriation by the finder was or was not theft, namely, whether the finder took the property knowing who the owner was, or having reasonable grounds for believing that he could be found. "Qui alienam rem adtrectavit, cum id se invito domino facere judicare deberet, furti tenetur. Sed si non fuit derelictum putavit tamen derelictum, furti non tenetur" (Sabin ap. Gell, l. c. § 20).

Under the Empire, as I have already mentioned, the general principle was adopted that anyone who could maintain a civil action for theft could, if he preferred to do so, prosecute the thief criminally. The penal action of theft was thus transformed into the Criminal trial, and was gradually superseded by the latter. In the time of Justinian, civil actions for theft were rare, as they could not be maintained at the same time as a Criminal prosecution. "Nunc furti plerumque criminaliter agi" (*D.* 47. 2. 92). The question may naturally be asked how it arose that an offence like theft, which is generally one of the earliest recognized as belonging to the Criminal Law, remained for such a long period a matter of a civil nature. The expla-

(*a*) The case supposed, though not larceny at Common Law, would probably be held to be larceny by a bailee under the Statute 24 & 25 Vict. c. 96, s. 3. See *R.* v. *Reeves*, 5 Jur. 716.

nation is to be found, I think, in the severity of the ancient Roman Law of debt, as well as in the other general causes which retarded the development of the Criminal Law at Rome. If the thief was not in a position to pay the value demanded by the injured party and approved of by the Judge, he was assigned by the Judge to the person from whom he had stolen as a bondsman (*a*). Thieves are not usually found among the wealthier classes; so in a large proportion of cases theft at Rome was punished even under the civil law by permanent loss of liberty.

Robbery was not in the early law distinguished from theft. A person guilty of this offence could always be proceeded against as for theft, *manifestum* or *nec manifestum*, according to the circumstances of his detection. The *actio vi bonorum raptorum* was first instituted, as Cicero tells us (pro Tullio, 8), by Lucullus in B.C. 77, by reason of the frequency of crimes of violence at that time. The penalty was triple the value of the property taken. It is improbable that it was ever used except when the offence did not come within the definition of *furtum manifestum;* and the principles applicable in reference to it were very much the same as in the case of theft.

The *actio damni injuria ex Lege Aquilia* is not properly speaking an action *ex delicto* at all, but one *quasi ex delicto.* It was not purely penal, like the actions *furti*, *injuriarum*, and *vi bonorum raptorum*, but mixed, the damages being assessed not on the principle of punishing the wrongdoer, but of compensating the party injured. It was the first true action of tort in the Roman system.

Injuria was an offence against the person, as distinguished from the other three delicts which dealt with offences against property. It was a comprehensive term, defined by Mr. Moyle (Just. Inst., p. 519, note) as a wilful violation of what writers on jurisprudence term the primordial rights of a free man—the rights to personal freedom, safety, and reputation. Assaults of all kinds, libels, slanders, violent abuse in public (*convicium*), illegal seizure for the purpose of annoyance, solicitation.

(*a*) See Mommsen, *Hist. Rome*, i. 160.

"Generaliter injuria dicitur omne quod non jure fit: specialiter alias contumelia." (Just. Inst. 4, 4, par.) The penalty was originally retaliation, then a sum fixed by law in each case, and finally such damages as the *Praetor* or *Judex* should assess (Gaius, iii. § 220–225) (*a*). Under the Empire *Injuriæ* were usually punished criminally. One of the Leges Corneliæ passed by Sulla in B.C. 81 specially dealt with the offence. This was before the general rule was adopted that every delict could be proceeded against criminally.

Such is a short summary of the Roman Law of Delicts. Viewing it as a substitute for the Criminal Law, we are struck at once by a notable omission. There is no penalty provided for the *death* of a free man. For a wound or a hurt not causing death, an *actio injuriæ* would lie; for the death of a slave an *actio damni injuriæ ex lege Aquilia*. But for the wilful homicide of a free man there was apparently no remedy. The reason of this we learn incidentally from the rules as to the *actio quasi ex delicto*, which was called *de effusis vel dejectis*. If, through the carelessness of a slave or otherwise, anything fell from a house and caused damage, a remedy *in duplum* was in general provided by this form of action; but if thereby a free man lost his life, a fixed penalty of 50 aurei was imposed, the reason given being that no estimation could be formed of the value of a free man's life. "Cum homo liber periit, damni æstimatio non fit in duplum (quia in homine libero nulla corporis æstimatio fieri potest) sed quinquaginta aureorem condemnatio fit" (*D.* 9. 3. 1. 5).

In other cases apparently there was no civil remedy for the death of a relative. If there had been it would have been a distinct exception to the rule that penal actions did not pass to the heir, and would have been mentioned as such. The rule in our own law prior to the passing of Lord Campbell's Act, 9 & 10 Vic. c. 93, was the same in this respect. The preamble to that Act commences:—"Whereas no action at law is now maintainable against a person who, by his wrongful act, neglect, or default,

(*a*) Poste, p. 474.

may have caused the death of another person, and it is oftentimes right and expedient that the wrongdoer in such cases shall be answerable in damages for the injury so caused by him." The Act then provides a remedy for the benefit of the wife, husband, child, or parent (*a*).

The theory of both systems of Law is that the value of human life is too great to be estimated in money. Life is too sacred to be atoned for otherwise than by the most severe punishment. At Rome the life of a citizen was always regarded with peculiar sanctity; and this may account for the absence of any trace of the death fine in the early law. In the Levitical Law the acceptance of such was positively forbidden on this very ground; and in all probability the same prohibition was enforced in early times at Rome.

What, then, was the early Roman Law of Homicide? We have surprisingly little information on the subject. The existing fragments of the XII. Tables contain no reference to homicide, though it is stated by Pliny (*b*) that, under this code, the penalty of death was awarded for the crime. This may, however, only have been a recognition of the right of private vengeance, as it was provided in the case of a limb being broken: "Si membrum rupit, ni cum eo pacit, talio esto." It is, however, stated in the *Digest* that the XII. Tables provided for the existence of *Quæstores Parricidii.* "Quæstores constituebantur a populo, qui capitalibus rebus præessent: hi appellabantur *quæstores parricidii*: quorum etiam meminit Lex XII. Tabularum." (*D.* 1. 2. 2. 23). It may be doubtful whether these "trackers of murder," as Mommsen calls them, were actually in existence at the date of the XII. Tables as here stated, but there can be no doubt that they were appointed at a very early date. They acted as a sort of police, their duties being to search for and arrest all murderers; *Parricidium* being apparently used to denote murder in general, not alone the murder of a parent or ascendant.

(*a*) But not for any other person. See *Osborne* v. *Gillet*, L. R. 8 Exch. 88.
(*b*) *Hist. Nat.* xviii. 3.

The appointment of these *Quæstores Parricidii* must be considered the first step in the creation of Criminal Law at Rome, as it involved a system of judicial inquiry and prosecution by the State; but as there was in all cases a right of appeal to the people in case of capital condemnation—a right which would naturally be very generally exercised, the Quæstores were rather in the position of magistrates conducting a preliminary inquiry, than of criminal judges. Whether their appointment did or did not immediately put an end to the system of private vengeance we cannot now tell. At all events we know that the punishment for homicide in the early law was death. At a later period of the Republic it was confiscation of goods, and banishment. How the system of capital punishment disappeared from the penal system of Republican Rome has been explained by Sir H. Maine. (*a*) It was revived by the legislation of Sulla about 81 B.C. The *Lex Cornelia de siccariis et beneficiis* punished murder whether committed by a weapon or poisoning, and also all attempts to murder. (Just. Inst 4, 18. 5). Under this law it appears that accessories were punished as severely as principals. (Cod. 9, 16. 7). The punishment was either death or banishment (*aqua et ignis interdictio*) (*D.* 48. 8. 3. 5).

Killing by negligence was not within the *Lex Cornelia.* In order to constitute the offence of homicide it was necessary that there should be an *intention* to kill, or at least to inflict a grievous wound. "Eum qui hominem occidit, si non occidendi animo hoc admisit absolvi posse. Et qui hominem non occidit sed vulneravit ut occidat pro homicida damnandum" (*D.* 48. 8. 1. 3).

The details of the law of homicide were very much like those of our own law. Nevertheless, as remarked by Mr. Justice Stephen (*b*), "The curious points which English lawyers have considered with so much care as to the nature of the connexion necessary to constitute homicide between the act causing death and the death caused by it do not seem to have

(*a*) *Ancient Law*, p. 387, et seq. (*b*) *Hist. Crim. Law*, i. 18.

occurred to the Roman lawyers, but there are various passages in the *Digest* which state the principal cases in which the intentional infliction of death was considered justifiable. They are all reducible to the cases of self-defence, and the arrest or punishment of criminals."

The Criminal Law of Rome may then be said to have originated in the legislation of Sulla. Prior to this, indeed, in the single case of homicide, the State appears to have punished as an offence against itself, an injury to one of its members, but this did not imply any regular system of Criminal Law. Nor was there any permanent Criminal tribunal in existence until in the year 149 B.C., the first *Quæstio Perpetua* was appointed by the *Lex Calpurnia de Repetundis.* This law, however, dealt only with a political offence, viz. extortion by Colonial Governors. Sulla's legislation, a little more than half a century later, covered the whole field of Criminal Law. In the matter of criminal procedure he adopted and extended the principle of the *Lex Calpurnia de Repetundis.* He instituted at least seven *Quæstiones* in addition to that *de repetundis*, viz. for Treason (*De Majestate*), for Injuries to the person or Insults (*De vi et injuriis*), for Murder (*Inter Sicarios*), for Bribery (*De ambitu*), for Fraud (*De Falsis*), for Embezzlement (*De peculatu*), for Adultery (*De Adulteris*). From the sentences of these Courts there was no appeal to the people. Their introduction, properly speaking, marks the birth of true Criminal Law. "From this Sullan legislation," says Mommsen (*a*), "dates the distinction—substantially unknown to the earlier law—between civil and criminal causes in the sense which we now attach to these expressions; henceforth a criminal cause appears as that which comes before a bench of jurymen (viz. a *Quæstio*), a civil cause as that which comes before the individual *Judex.* The whole body of the Sullan ordinances as to the Quæstiones may be characterized at once as the first Roman Code after the XII. Tables, and as the first criminal code specially issued at all."

(*a*) *Hist. of Rome*, book iv., chap. 10.

From the time of Sulla forward criminal legislation was abundant; until, after the establishment of the Empire, not only was there a large body of Statute Criminal Law, but what we would in English Law designate as Common Law criminal offences came into existence; the general rule having been adopted that anyone against whom an action *ex delicto* would lie for *furtum*, *vi bonorum raptorum*, or *injuria*, might at the option of the injured person be prosecuted criminally instead.

Why was it, then, that the Roman Law, which was so rapid in its development on the civil side, was so slow in attaining to a system of criminal jurisprudence? For this there were, I think, three main reasons:—(1) The form of government; (2) The essentially irreligious character of the people; and (3) The existence of slavery.

In the first place the Republican form of government, greatly hindered the development of Criminal Law. We see, in the history of early English Criminal Law, what a large share the existence of the monarchy had in its creation. An offence against one of his subjects became an offence against the King himself. The extension of the Criminal Law, administered by the King personally or his deputies, strengthened and secured the Monarchy enormously, while it gave to his subjects the blessings of peace and security.

The Republican spirit, on the other hand, is very much opposed to the growth of Criminal Law. It is usually jealous of the recognition of any authority for punishment except the supreme will of the people: and so we find that at Rome, during the Republic, in every capital case there was an appeal to the people. The cause was discussed always in three public assemblies before it was finally decided. The magistrate who had given judgment was obliged to appear and defend his sentence, and in this manner occupied the position of a public prosecutor rather than that of a judge. It was not until the fourth meeting that the question as to the verdict was put. "In this way," says Mommsen, "the Roman criminal procedure was completely void of principle, and was degraded into the sport and instrument of political parties" (*a*). Every great crime became a party question. The result is well described by Cicero. "Plura enim multo, homines judicant odio aut amore aut cupiditate, aut iracundia, aut dolore, aut lætitia, aut spe, aut timore, aut errore, aut aliqua permotione mentis, quam veritate, aut præscripto, aut juris norma aliqua, aut judicii formula aut legibus" (*b*). A criminal trial thus quickly degenerated into a party broil; and to this, probably more than to any other cause, is to be traced the decline of the Roman Republic. Let us hope that Democratic government may not produce the same result with us. The appeal from a Judge and Jury to "the Press of the United Kingdom," which has now become usual in every case of capital condemnation, seems to promise us very much the same result. It may have been with a view to checking disorder, and not as supposed by Mommsen with the object of putting an end to capital punishment, that C. Gracchus in 123 B.C. attempted to withdraw the cognizance of murder and poisoning from the popular assemblies altogether and to entrust it to permanent judicial commissions. This reform was actually carried out by Sulla a short time afterwards.

The absence of any religious element is one of the most strongly-marked features of the Roman Law; and the growth of Criminal Law was greatly checked by this characteristic. The first offences which the community as such punishes are usually what it regards as grievous sins, or wrongs of such a particularly heinous nature that religion forbids that they should be compounded for merely by a money payment. That this was so in the history of English Criminal Law appears plainly from the extract from the writings of King Alfred, quoted by Sir H. Maine, in the last chapter of his "Ancient Law." (*c*). The Romans, on the contrary, as regards the first class of offences, adopted the cynical principle that it was a matter for the gods themselves to revenge insults offered to them; and as

(*a*) *Hist. of Rome*, book ii., chap. 8. (*b*) *De Orat.* (ii. 42, 178).
(*c*) p. 398.

regards offences against man, they were not restrained by any religious considerations, except apparently in the one case of homicide, from allowing the injury to be atoned for by a money payment to the person injured.

The third cause of the slow development of Criminal Law in Rome was the existence of slavery. Crimes are generally committed by the lowest class of the population, which, in a State which recognizes slavery, is chiefly composed of slaves; and the law does not as a rule deal with slaves except through their masters, who are civilly responsible for their acts, and who have ample power of inflicting punishment themselves. On this account the want of a Criminal Law was not much felt at Rome, until, under the influence of Christianity, the power of masters to take the lives of their slaves was taken away, and slavery gradually ceased to exist.

These were, I think, the main causes which retarded the growth of Criminal Law in the Roman system, and which rendered the Roman Law a marked contrast to modern legal systems in respect to the relative importance of its criminal and civil branches.

LECTURE V.

EARLY ENGLISH PENAL LAW.

AT the present day, as Sir Henry Maine remarks (*a*), two systems of law divide between them the whole civilized world—one is the Roman Law, which forms the foundation of the legal system prevailing throughout Continental Europe, the other is the English Law, which practically rules the whole new world as well as the United Kingdom. In my last Lecture I briefly sketched the origin and development of Criminal Law at Rome: I now come to our own system, the history of which is, in many respects, even more interesting to the student of general jurisprudence, and of course much more important to those who intend to devote themselves to the practice of law in this country; for our modern Criminal Law has retained many of the features which it exhibited in very early times, and a knowledge of its history is absolutely essential in order to understand its principles. Its history is continuous from the earliest origin of the Anglo-Saxon race to the present day. There was no break at the Norman Conquest as is commonly supposed. The Norman kings administered the Saxon Law, and merely took the place of their Saxon predecessors in the administration of justice as in the performance of the other duties of government.

The laws of the Anglo-Saxons were, as might naturally be

(*a*) *Early Law and Custom*, p. 165.

expected, almost identical with those of other German tribes; for the Saxon invaders of Britain brought with them all the customs of their forefathers. The primitive method for the punishment of crimes with them as with other nations was merely vengeance. Each individual protected his own rights and avenged his own wrongs by whatever power he himself possessed, and in the manner in which he himself thought best. At this stage of legal progress Courts of Justice did not exist; and there is nothing that we can properly term Law in existence, no rule or limitation as to the right of vengeance except the powers of the person injured to exact it, and the power of his enemy to resist. "It is," in the words of Mr. Laughlin (*a*), "one of the most instructive lessons in the history of English Law to trace the growth of the power of government over the individual; the establishment of Courts of Justice; the gradual suppression of private warfare; the substitution of permanent kings for temporary leaders; and in the course of time, the assumption by the king of the 'ideal attributes of absolute perfection, absolute immortality, and legal ubiquity.'"

We do not find the *lex talionis* established as the principle of early German Law. In so far as it existed it was only a limitation of the right of revenge. It was allowable to inflict mutilation of one kind in revenge for mutilation of another kind, provided the punishment was not excessive, but the gravity of the offence was the measure of the punishment. The first germ of legal procedure is here found in an *ex post facto* investigation by the community into the act of vengeance whatever it was, with a view to deciding whether the revenge taken was reasonable or not, according to this test. Thus, by the laws of Ina, it was provided that anyone who had slain a thief should take an oath of his guilt, and that in that way he should escape liability for his act. "Qui furem occiderit, debet inventare cum juramento, quod illum culpabilem et de vita forisfactum occidisset, et non solvat" (Ina, 16).

And by the laws of Henry I. (really a summary of the

(*a*) *Essays on Anglo-Saxon Law*, p. 262.

existing Saxon Laws) it was enacted:—"If anyone kill another in revenge or self-defence, let him take to himself none of the goods of the dead, neither his horse, nor helmet, nor sword, nor any money; but in wonted manner let him arrange the body of the dead—his head to the west, his feet to the east—upon his shield, if he have it; and let him drive deep his lance, and hang there his arms, and to it rein in his steed; and let him go to the nearest vill, and to him whom he shall first meet, as well as to him who has *socn*, let him declare it, that he may have proof and make defence against his (the slain man's) kinsmen and friends" (83, § 6).

The right of revenge is here recognized, in the same manner as that of self-defence. Even if the criminal escaped and was taken by some other person, the right of vengeance remained, and he was delivered to the relatives for the purpose of exacting it. This is put beyond doubt by a passage from the Laws of Canute (ii. 56): "Qui murdrum aperte perpetrabit, reddatur parentibus interfecti" (*Leges Knut.* ii. 56). This system of private vengeance of course led to terrible anarchy. The offender was often as strong as, if not stronger than, his adversary; and the assistance of the kinsmen on each side created a blood-feud, lasting perhaps for generations, out of a single crime. But in the evolution of law remedy was at length found.

The great step towards the limitation of the right of private vengeance was the introduction of pecuniary compositions for offences. The acceptance of such was originally, it is safe to assume, purely voluntary, the offender buying off revenge at such a price as the person injured might choose to accept in consideration of foregoing his right to it. There is, no doubt, that in the Brehon Law this system of composition was at first purely voluntary; and though there is no direct authority that it was so in the Anglo-Saxon system, there are passages in the laws which seem to imply it. Thus, by the laws of Æthelbert, it is provided:—(65) "If a thigh be broken, let bōt be made with 12 sh.; if the man become halt, *then the friends must arbi-*

trate"(*a*). We have under the Brehon Laws many instances of persons who had slain others *endeavouring to persuade* the relatives to accept a composition, and sometimes succeeding and sometimes not (*b*). There is no doubt therefore that in that system the decision rested, not with any legal authority, but with the parties injured or their friends. Probably this was also the case under Anglo-Saxon Law.

When once the system of compositions was established everything tended to extend it. The influence of Christianity by teaching mildness and forbearance; the influence of the government, when a settled government was once instituted, in seeking to check disorder; and finally, the manifest advantages, both to the wrongdoer and the injured parties of preventing a resort to bloodshed. These considerations led in time to an actual enforcement of the system. The first criminal legislation in England consisted merely of an ordinance by the king forbidding the resort to vengeance before an effort was made to obtain pecuniary composition for the wrong. To enforce this command required not only the sanction of public opinion, but also some real authority in the sovereign.

When Alfred held the throne he was sufficiently strong to carry out this policy, and to forbid a resort to vengeance unless a claim for compensation were first made. The following is his enactment on the subject:—

"Also, we decree that the man who knows his foe to be home-sitting shall not fight him before he asks satisfaction.

"If he have power to surround and besiege his foe let him watch him during seven days, and not attack him if he wish to remain there. If he wish to surrender and give up his arms let him guard him unhurt thirty days, and announce it to his kinsmen and his friends (*c*).

(*a*) Thorpe, *Ancient Laws, &c., of England*, p. 8. Compare the provision of the XII. Tables (quoted, *ante*, p. 60). Si membrum rupit *ni cum eo pacit* talio esto.

(*b*) See *ante*, p. 27.

(*c*) Apparently with the object of enabling them to assist in making up the required amount of composition.

"If he have not power to besiege him within, let him go to the ealdorman and ask aid; if he be unwilling to aid him, let him go to the king before he attack his foe" (*Laws of Alfred*, § 42, pr. § 1-3).

This passage is interesting, not only as showing the nature of the fine or composition paid, but also by its reference to the position of the king in the matter. He is not a judge. He is merely a referee of the justice of vengeance. This is probably the first recognition in the laws of the necessity of any application to the sovereign before the right of private vengeance was enforced. We will see how, from this first beginning, the king gradually increased his authority, chiefly availing himself, in order to do so, of the plea that an unauthorized act of vengeance was a violation of his peace. It was not, however, until long after the Conquest that the king, by means of this plea, attracted to himself the whole criminal jurisdiction, and finally put an end to private warfare and private revenge.

We have in Modern English Law one rule which is probably a survival of the right of private revenge. One of the cases mentioned by Alfred in which private vengeance was justifiable, was where a husband found a man with his wife under circumstances which would justify him in supposing that they were together for the purpose of committing adultery. "A man may fight 'orwige' [*i. e.* without committing war] if he find another with his lawful wife within closed doors, or under one covering, or with his lawfully born daughter, or with his lawfully born sister, or with his mother, who was given to his father as his lawful wife" (*Laws of Alfred*, § 42). Modern Law recognizes the provocation in this case to a certain extent. It treats the killing of an adulterer taken in the act in the same way as if he had been killed in a quarrel. The killing is not indeed held to be *justifiable*, but it is laid down that the provocation reduces the crime from murder to manslaughter. (Hale, *Pleas of the Crown*, i. 486, R. *v.* Kelly, 2 C. & K. 814.) This is, I believe, the only case in which provocation, other than by actual blows, is considered sufficient to reduce homicide to manslaughter, if the killing be effected with a deadly weapon.

The compensation which was paid for homicide under Anglo-Saxon Law was threefold—

(1) The *wer*, which was the regular price of a man fixed according to his rank, and which was paid to his relatives in case of his death. This was purely a *personal* value estimated according to a man's rank and position.

(2) The *bot*, also paid to the relatives as compensation for the crime. This varied according to the *nature of the act*. In case of theft, it amounted to the value of the goods stolen. It was also paid as a satisfaction for an injury to honour or health, or such injuries to the person as inflicted no pecuniary loss. The term is derived from the same root as our modern word "better."

(3) The *wite*, a fine paid to the king as a penalty for the breach of his peace. This, as we shall afterwards see, was the origin of royal jurisdiction in criminal matters. The right of a person to be undisturbed in his dwelling by an act of violence committed near it, is one early recognized by the law. The higher the rank the greater the distance to which this right extends, and ultimately it comes in the case of the sovereign to include the whole kingdom.

This system of fines is recognized as the sole punishment for offences throughout the Anglo-Saxon Laws, unless we consider the primitive revenge, which under certain conditions, was always permitted a punishment.

The imposition of the fine in serious cases was always discretionary with the injured party, who might refuse to accept it, and insist on his right of revenge. "If a thief be seized let him perish by death, or let his life be redeemed according to his wēr" (*Laws of Ina*). In the case of murder the option of accepting or refusing pecuniary compensation lay with the nearest relatives of the deceased. The guilty person was delivered over to the relatives, who might kill him or spare him as they thought fit, exacting in the latter case the customary fine. This clearly appears from the Laws of King Henry I. In Chapter LXXI, "De Homicidio vel aliis maleficiis," the following passage occurs :—

"Si quis veneno, vel sortilegio, vel invultucione, seu maleficio aliquo, faciat homicidium, sive illi paratum sit sive alii, nichil refert, quin factum mortiferum, et nullo modo redimentum sit. *Reddatur utique qui fuerit reus hujusmodi parentibus et amicis interfecti, ut eorum misericordiam aut judicium senciat, quibus ipse non pepercit.* Si res in compellacione sit, et emundacione miseveniat, episcopi judicio reservetur. Et si beneficio legis ad misericordiam vel concordiam pertrahatur, de wera mortui plene satisfaciat; et witam, et manbotam, et, omnibus rite pacatis, plegios legalitatis deinceps inveniat: triplex vero lada vel emundacio in agendis hujusmodi sit."

The rule in the case of injuries not causing death is next stated :—"Si autem insorticatus non fuerit mortuus, sed cutis variacionem vel probabilem corporis contrahat egritudinem, emendetur, sapientum antiquis diffinicionibus, sicut acciderit." In this latter case apparently vengeance was not permitted. Nor was it allowed in cases of homicide by misadventure.

When the Monarchy grew in strength, the King sought to preserve order in his dominions by enforcing the acceptance of fines, and prohibiting revenge, unless the injured person had previously offered to accept pecuniary compensation. The extent to which revenge was permitted varied in different reigns, according as the King's authority prevailed. Thus, although by the laws of Henry I. revenge was justified, it was forbidden by laws of *Ina.* The "Leges Henrici Primi" were not, as I have already stated, a regular code established by that King, but rather a compilation of the existing Anglo-Saxon Laws by some unknown author. Consequently in many respects they are more archaic than earlier codes. Thus, although they sanctioned revenge in every case of serious injury, it was provided by the laws of King Ina, that if anyone took revenge before he demanded justice, he should give up what he had taken to himself, and pay the damage done, and make bōt with xxx shillings.

It was not until long after the Conquest, that this system of private revenge ceased. The King's Courts gradually grew powerful; and finally, by the Statute of Marlbridge (52 Hen. III. cap. 1), it was made a finable offence to exact revenge or enforce the payment of compensation in lieu thereof without the intervention of a court of law. That statute commences by reciting that "whereas at the time of a commotion late stirred up within this realm, and also sithence, many great men, and divers other, have disdained to be justised by the King and his Court, like as they ought and were wont in time of the King's noble progenitors, and also in his time, but took great revenges and distresses of their neighbours, and of other, until they had amends and fines at their own pleasure." It then provides that "none from henceforth shall take any such revenge or distress of his own authority without award of our Court, though he have damage or injury whereby he would have amends of his neighbour either higher or lower." And it further enacts, "that if any from henceforth take such revenges of his own authority, without award of the King's Court as before is said, and be convict thereof, he shall be punished by fine, and that according to the trespass." Henceforth self-redress was entirely forbidden in English Law, except in a few specified cases. An injury inflicted in revenge for another is treated in all respects as if it were an unprovoked trespass.

The prohibition of revenge, even although it were only until after demand made for pecuniary satisfaction, necessarily implied some means of enforcing the payment of fines; for otherwise the offender could by flight entirely baffle his adversary. Hence arose the system of outlawry. A person who refused to pay the accustomed satisfaction, and sought safety in flight, was declared an outlaw, and thereby punished for his offence.

Outlawry was the punishment for non-payment of fines in all systems of law, and forms the connecting link between private Penal Law and true Criminal Law. The sentence was pronounced at the County Court, which, with the Anglo-Saxons corresponded to the tribal assembly of other nations. It was necessary that the accused should be called at four successive Courts, and if he failed to appear, he was then declared an outlaw at the fifth. The effect of the sentence was to deprive the outlaw of all rights as regards person or property. He was really placed *outside the law* in every respect. He could be killed with impunity by any person who met him. He lost all his property, moveable and immoveable. He could not demand payment of fines for any injury done to him. He lost his wergeld, as the Irishman lost his honour-price.

The punishment of outlawry, though originally a means merely of enforcing the payment of fines, continued to exist long after the system of fines had disappeared. In fact it is theoretically recognized in our Criminal Law to the present day, though practically it has long become obsolete (see Blackstone, *Commentaries*, iv., chap. 24).

The importance of outlawry as a punishment in early times may be estimated by the space which is occupied in discussing it in early treatises on Criminal Law. Bracton, in his work *De Corona*, most minutely specifies the requirements necessary before sentence of outlawry can be pronounced; and the effect of such sentence when imposed upon any person. Chapter XI. of that work deals with outlawry, and provides in what manner an accused person is to be summoned before sentence of outlawry is pronounced:—

"When indeed any person has so withdrawn himself on account of homicide or any other crime, by the beneficence and grace of the prince he shall be called to come and make answer, and to stand on his defence, if there is anyone who will speak against him; otherwise he is not to be forthwith called without the suit of someone, because when grave crimes are charged against an absent defendant, sentence is not usually hastened, but he is accustomed to be called that he may be required, not indeed for punishment, but that he may have the power to purge himself, if he can purge himself, and a legitimate time shall be allowed to him, namely five months, that is within the fifth County [Court] to stand on his defence, and to answer to the accuser concerning the crime imputed to him; but if he should not have come within that time, he shall be held to be an outlaw, since he does not obey the prince nor the law, and he shall be thenceforth declared an outlaw, like him who is out of the law, Laughelesman [Lawless-man]" (*a*).

He then goes on to say that a person is not to be declared an outlaw unless he has been pursued by some person entitled to exact reparation from him :—

"But when a malefactor has taken flight, there ought to be someone to follow the fugitive, to speak from sight and hearing that he is a fugitive (*b*), ... and let him then state all the words of the charge as if the fugitive were present, and let him in the charge, and his accusation, add that if he shall see the person charged, he shall speak against him. But to make this kind of suit let not any one of the people be admitted unless it appertains to him by relationship to pursue him, by reason that he is of blood and relationship connected with the slain person, and in which case when there are several accusers, the nearest relation is always preferred to the more remote."

It is the "avenger of blood" according to the language of the old Hebrew Law who alone in case of murder can enforce the outlawry. No substitute was allowed to be appointed. The duty of pursuit was sacred. "No person ought to pursue to outlawry for another, unless it be for a person slain, so connected by relationship or homage, that if the accused party were present, an appeal would lie between them" (*c*).

(*a*) Bracton, *De Legibus Angliae.* Twiss's translation, vol. ii. p. 309.

(*b*) The oath "de visu et auditu" (Glanville, p. 2, c. 3) was abolished by Stat. West. I. chap. 41 (3 Ed. I.).

(*c*) Bracton, vol. ii. p. 313.

An outlaw forfeited by his outlawry all his rights. "Likewise the outlaw forfeits every benefit which belongs to the peace of the King, because from the time when he is outlawed he carries a wolf's head, so that he may be killed by everyone with impunity, particularly if he defends himself or takes to flight, so that his capture is difficult" (*a*). He loses his property, and forfeits "everything which is of right or possession, of right accruing or likely to accrue, of right acquired or to be acquired, and all possession in like manner in the form and mode of possessing."

A person outlawed might, however, be inlawed by the grace of the King, and admitted to the King's peace (chap. xiv.). "But a person inlawed is not restored to anything but the King's peace, for the King cannot grant a pardon with injury or damage to others [non enim poterit rex gratiam facere, cum injuria et damno aliorum]. He is therefore not restored to his rights of action or property which he has lost by outlawry" (*b*) (chap. xiv.).

Such, apparently, was the manner in which personal revenge for offences became transformed into a system of pecuniary fines, the payment of which was enforced by outlawry. We have now to inquire into the manner in which the system of fines was in its turn superseded by a regular system of punishments.

In considering the various causes which led to the disappearance of the fines in our own legal system, we must in the first place bear in mind that it was always considered as an indulgence to an offender to allow him to escape the consequence of his crime by making a money payment. The Anglo-Saxon Laws required an injured person to accept the accustomed payment in most cases, but this rule was never universal. Thus in case of a second offence by the same person, the acceptance of a fine was never enforced. "At the first time," says a law of Ethelred, "let him make *bot* to the accuser, and

(*a*) *Ibid.*, p. 339. (*b*) *Ibid.*, p. 371.

to the lord his *wer*, and let him give true *borhs* that he will hereafter abstain from all evil. And at the second time let there be no other *bot* than the head" (*a*).

Certain crimes also, in consequence of their enormity, were always considered incapable of being compensated for by money. Thus, the Laws of Cnut declare that "Housebreaking and arson, and open theft, and open-morth, and treason against a lord are by the secular law *bot*-less" (*b*). The imposition of fines had thus only a limited range at any time, and many causes tended to still further restrict it.

The first of these was the influence of religion. Curiously enough, Christianity helped both the growth and the decline of the system of pecuniary fines. It assisted its establishment as a mitigation of the terrible system of private revenge for wrongs. To accept pecuniary satisfaction was always looked upon as an act of forbearance. This clearly appears from the account given in the *Senchus Mor*, of the establishment of the Eric fines which I quoted in a previous lecture (*c*). It was, as the commentator in that work calls it, "a middle course between forgiveness and retaliation." Probably the same view was taken by the Anglo-Saxon Church, which consequently encouraged the system. But once regularly established, the fines came to be looked upon as a *punishment* rather than as the price of forgiveness; and as moral ideas became developed, the fines appeared to be in many cases a most inadequate punishment.

In so far as the offence committed was a *sin*, the Church then discouraged the idea that it could be atoned for by money alone. The passage from the writings of King Alfred, quoted by Sir H. Maine (*Ancient Law*, p. 398) clearly indicates the growth of this idea. "After this it happened that many nations received the faith of Christ, and there were many synods assembled throughout the earth, and among the English race also after they had received the faith of Christ, both of holy bishops and of their exalted Witan. They then ordained

(*a*) Thorpe, i. 281. (*b*) Thorpe, i. 411. (*c*) *ante*, p.

that out of that mercy which Christ had taught, secular lords, with their leave, might without sin take for every misdeed the *bot* in money which they ordained; except in cases of treason against a lord, to which they dared not assign any mercy, because Almighty God adjudged none to them that despised Him, nor did Christ adjudge any to them which sold Him to death; and He commanded that a lord should be loved like Himself."

Here the acceptance of the fine is plainly regarded as *primâ facie* wrong. It is only *permitted* by the Church in the case of lesser offences, and condemned in the case of more heinous crimes. The same idea which led the Hebrews to condemn the acceptance of a death fine as a grievous sin, gradually put an end to the *weregeld* in England also.

Another cause for the disappearance of the fines was the system of frankpledge. By means of the latter, the imposition of fines was gradually transformed into a most effective police organization. According to the system of frankpledge, as established in the 10th and 11th centuries, all men were bound to combine themselves in groups of tens, each of whom was responsible for the acts of the others. If one committed an offence the others were bound to arrest him and deliver him over to justice, or make good the mischief which the offender had done. Even to the present day there are remnants of this system in English Law, though for centuries it has had no practical operation (*a*).

There can be no doubt, I think, that frankpledge was a survival of the system of tribal responsibility for crime which prevailed almost universally at an early stage of legal progress, and of which we find in the Brehon Laws the most complete and elaborate code. There always coexisted with this responsibility, wherever it prevailed, a right to surrender a criminal in lieu of being answerable for his acts; such, for instance, appears to have been the origin of the *noxæ deditio* of the Roman Law.

(*a*) See Stephen's *History of Criminal Law*, i. 66.

The organization of hundreds and tithings in the Anglo-Saxon system originated, in all probability, in this family liability; and when in the progress of society the gradual break-up of the family system took place, frankpledge survived. The tribal liability was thus transformed into a system of compelling the hundred under penalty of a fine to seek for, arrest, and produce a criminal. The change was of course complete long before Bracton wrote, but the account which he gives of the matter plainly indicates the origin of the system. The liability of the tithing to pay the fine which existed, even though the malefactor were caught and delivered over to justice, if he were not delivered over by the tithing itself, shows that it was not merely for the default in arresting him, as it is sometimes stated, that the fine was imposed. The account given by Bracton is so interesting that it is worth quoting at length. It is contained in chapter x. of his work, *De Corona*, and is as follows :—

" We have spoken of those who are present or may be seized in an act of felony done in public, several persons standing by and seeing it, as in some assemblies. But because there are some persons who forthwith betake themselves to flight after a felony and cannot be seized, let the hue be raised after them from vill to vill until the malefactors are captured, otherwise let the whole district be amerced to the King. . . . . . But concerning the person who has thus taken to flight, it will have to be diligently inquired if he was in frankpledge and in a tithing, and *then the tithing will be amerciable before our justices because they have not produced the malefactor for trial, although he has been captured again by others beforehand and delivered to prison, since he has not been captured and produced by the tithing.* But if he be out of frankpledge and received into some vill, the district of the vill will be amerciable, unless the person who has run away ought not to be in a tithing or in frankpledge ; as, for instance, magnates, knights, and their relations, a clerk, a freeman, and such like, according to the custom of the country, and in which case the person, of whose family and household he may be, will be liable in some parts, and he shall be responsible for them, unless the custom of the country introduces a different principle, that he ought not to be responsible for his household. . . . . . Because every man, whether free or a serf, either is or ought to be in frankpledge, or in somebody's household, unless he be somebody itinerant from place to place, who does not keep himself to one more than to another, or who has something which suffices for frankpledge, as a dignity, or an order, or a free tenement, or real property in a city. And according to the Laws of King Edward, everyone who is of the age of twelve ought to make oath at the view of frankpledge that he is not a robber nor will conspire with a robber; and every person who has land and house, who are called 'householders,' ought to be in frankpledge, and also others who serve them who are called 'followers,' for neither ought a person to repel from himself his servitor before he is purged from every charge of which he has been previously charged" (*a*).

But the main cause of the disappearance of the system of fines from our Criminal Law was the growth of Royal Jurisdiction in criminal matters. This opens up such a wide subject for inquiry that I must reserve what I have to say upon the matter for another Lecture.

(*a*) Bracton, *De Legibus Angliæ*, vol. ii., pp. 303–309.

LECTURE VI.

EARLY ENGLISH CRIMINAL LAW.

THE distinguishing feature of modern English Criminal Law is the fact that the Sovereign is in all cases the prosecuting party. The Queen prosecutes every petty larceny, and at the same time, by her delegate, the Judge of Assize tries the offender. Theoretically she is judge in her own cause, a position which is repugnant to every principle of jurisprudence.

What, then, is the origin in English Law of this prosecution by the Crown in all criminal matters? The answer of Blackstone and the Analytical School of Jurisprudence is simply that the King is the fountain of justice, and that he is bound to see that the law is enforced in the public interest. If this be so, why is the name of the Sovereign not used in civil actions? Surely it is as much in the public interest that the Civil Law should be enforced, as that the Criminal Law should be. The answer to the question is really historical. The prosecution by the Crown first arose not from any notion of public convenience, but in an entirely different way; and moreover our Criminal Law still retains traces of the manner in which the system originally grew up.

Every lawyer is familiar with the modern form of an indictment. The offence is always alleged to have been committed "against the peace of our Sovereign Lady the Queen, her

Crown and dignity." Until a very recent date, an indictment prepared without this formal ending was wholly bad. A recent statute, however (14 & 15 Vict. c. 100, s. 24), specially provides that an indictment is not to be held insufficient in consequence of the omission of the words "against the peace." Before it became law an indictment without these words was considered not to charge any offence, no matter how formal it was in every other respect. Why was this? The real reason was that the averment that every offence was "against the peace," which in time had become a mere formality, was originally the real statement of the crime with which the accused was charged. An investigation of the history of English Criminal Law shows that originally only a real violation of the King's personal rights was the subject of an indictment; and that the origin of our present system of criminal procedure was a proceeding to avenge an offence against the King personally, which he prosecuted in exactly the same manner as a private individual proceeded against one who had wronged him. The violation of the King's peace was an insult to him personally, and so was punished by him.

In nearly all ancient systems of law the violation of the peace of any chief or person of importance is recognized as an offence. Thus, we find elaborate provisions existing in the Ancient Irish Law as to the maiginn or "precinct" of a chief, and the penalties laid down for any violation of its sanctity. The Early English Laws contained similar provisions (*a*). An act of violence within the ambit of the King's or a lord's demesne was an offence against him, in the same manner as a violation of neutral territory is regarded as an offence by modern International Law. The King's peace first extended only to the particular place where he happened to be; and to such places as had this special privilege conferred upon them (*b*).

"The King's presence," says Sir F. Palgrave, "imparted

(*a*) See Stephen's, *History of Criminal Law*, i. 60.

(*b*) *Ibid.*, 60 (note).

peace, not only to his residence, but to a considerable district around it. Three miles, three furlongs, and three acre-breadths, nine feet, nine palms, and three barley-corns, constituted the mystical radius of the verge, which was reckoned from the town or mansion where the King held his Court; and within this ambit the protection by royalty was to remain unviolated. At certain times and holidays also, the King's peace was to be observed throughout the realm. The week of the ceremony of the coronation constituted one of these privileged periods: they also recurred periodically at the three great festivals of the year, Christmas, Easter, and Whitsuntide, being the several seasons when the King wore his crown in the great Councils of the respective Anglo-Saxon States or Kingdoms. Lastly, the King's peace could be 'given' by his word and will, by his 'hand' or by his writ, or by his seal; and the punishment of the transgressor was greatly enhanced if he violated the protection thus afforded. In some shires the breach of the King's peace, or violation, or contempt of the royal authority, increased the mulcts paid by the offender; in others it placed his life and limbs at the King's mercy, or exposed him to the dread penalty of outlawry, rendering him guilty of a capital crime, which was visited by the extreme rigour of the law. Sometime after the Conquest, all these special protections were disused: but they were replaced by a general proclamation of the 'King's peace,' which was made when the community assented to the accession of the new Monarch; and this first proclamation was considered to be in force during the remainder of his life, so as to bring any disturber of the public tranquillity within its penalties. So much importance was attached to the ceremonial act of the proclamation, that, even in the reign of John, offences committed during the interregnum, or period elapsing between the day of the death of the last Monarch and the recognition of his successor, were unpunishable in those tribunals whose authority was derived from the Crown" (Palgrave, *Rise and Progress of the English Commonwealth*, i. 284–5).

The original "pleas of the Crown" were either offences

against the King personally, such as treason or concealment of treasure-trove; or some act of violence committed in such a manner as really to amount to a breach of the peace. Theft, for instance, is not found in the list of pleas of the Crown given by Glanville, though robbery is, as it necessarily involved an act of violence. Gradually the system arose of *alleging* that an offence such as theft was committed "against the peace," even though accompanied by no violence whatsoever. By this means the prosecutor escaped the awkward incident which always attached to a proceeding by him personally, of being liable to be challenged by the accused to a trial by combat. It was laid down that the King should not fight, as such a course would be beneath his dignity, and consequently in prosecutions by him the accused could not claim a trial by combat.

The allegation of a violation of the King's peace thus gradually became a mere fictitious averment to confer jurisdiction; but for a long time a real distinction was made between cases where there was and where there was not a real breach of the King's peace. Thus in Britton's *Treatise*, written probably in the reign of Edward I, it is laid down in reference to larcenies, that there are two modes of procedure, either by the party from whom the goods are stolen or by the King, and it is stated on behalf of the King that when the wrongdoer has been sued in form of trespass by the owner of the goods the King will not proceed against him, *even though his peace may have been broken* (*a*).

The definition of murder given by Lord Coke (3 *Inst.* 47) shows a trace of the same idea: "when a person of sound memory and discretion unlawfully killeth any reasonable creature in being and *under the King's peace* with malice aforethought, either express or implied."

Probably also, this idea of a violation of the King's peace explains the strictly territorial limits of modern English Criminal Law. If an Englishman makes a contract with another in

(*a*) Britton, p. 118.

France, it may be enforced against him in an English Court, but if he steals his fellow-countryman's property there, he cannot be tried by an English tribunal! The "peace of our Sovereign Lady the Queen" is not affected by anything which takes place outside her own territory (*a*). This is not the only feature in our modern Criminal Law which is explained by its historical origin.

The gradual change from a system of private revenge or pecuniary compensation to a true system of Criminal Law was, as I have already shown (*b*), materially assisted by the growth of the royal power. When once the Sovereign became strong enough to preserve the peace, the reasons in favour of a system of fines for the sake of preserving order and putting an end to blood feuds ceased to exist, and fines entirely disappeared from our criminal system. The prosecution by the Crown in criminal matters finally disposed of the system of pecuniary compensation. It emphasized the growing idea that punishment, not revenge, was the object of the proceeding, for it was obvious to any person who took the trouble to consider the matter that the Sovereign was not really injured in any way, and that his motive for the proceeding must be more or less of a moral or utilitarian nature. In fact, the interposition of the Sovereign as a party, not merely as a judge, really effected the transformation from Penal Law to Criminal Law in our system.

It is not merely a matter of conjecture that the growth of Royal Jurisdiction as regards crimes gradually transformed our criminal system in the way I have stated. Royal prosecutions did not at once supersede prosecutions by the parties themselves. This was only a gradual process. All through the Middle Ages, and indeed long after that period is considered to have come to a close, two systems of prosecutions for crimes continued to exist side by side. Either the party aggrieved (or his relatives

(*a*) This is the general rule, but there are a few statutory exceptions. Treason (26 Hen. VIII. c. 15), murder (24 & 25 Vic. c. 100, s. 9), and bigamy (24 & 25 Vic. c. 100, s. 57), if committed abroad by British subjects, are indictable in England or Ireland. See Stephen's *History of Criminal Law*, ii. 13, *et seq.*

(*b*) See *ante*, pp. 81, 82.

in case of his death) might institute a proceeding (*a*) which was called an appeal, or, if he failed to do so, the Sovereign might take up the matter and prosecute for the violation of his peace. Gradually appeals became rarer and rarer, and at last entirely obsolete; but they were not formally abolished until the year 1819 (*b*). As long, however, as they continued to exist they retained all their primitive characteristics. The accused had the option of a trial by battle; and he could compound with his accuser by the payment of a pecuniary fine. When the King prosecuted, both these barbarous incidents disappeared. It was laid down by Bracton that the King did not give wager of battle; and it was obviously still more beneath his dignity to make a bargain for the life of a malefactor. As then we find that where the King did not prosecute, the acceptance of pecuniary compensation was always allowable, and when he did, it was not, we may safely assert, that the cause of the disappearance was the fact of the Crown prosecuting in nearly every case.

The history of this system of appeals is both interesting and instructive. When Blackstone wrote his Commentaries appeals were not entirely obsolete, and in his fourth volume he gives a short account of them. He defines an appeal as "an accusation by a private subject against another for some heinous crime, demanding punishment on account of the particular injury suffered, rather than for the offence against the public" (*c*).

"The chief object of an appeal at all times," he further states, "was to compel the defendant to make a pecuniary compensation. For when the verdict in an appeal was given in favour of the appellant, he might insist upon what terms he pleased as the ransom of the defendant's life, or a commutation of the sentence" (*d*). An appeal was in reality a survival of the

(*a*) It is scarcely necessary to point out that our modern private prosecutions have nothing to do with the ancient "Appeals." In private, as well as in public prosecutions the Crown is formally the prosecuting party.

(*b*) 59 Geo. III. c. 46.

(*c*) *Commentaries*, iv. 312.

(*d*) *Ibid.* 316 (note).

primitive mode of redress by revenge or pecuniary satisfaction. It corresponded exactly to the penal action of the Roman Law. It had very little resemblance to a criminal prosecution in the modern sense of the term, being rather akin to an action of tort. In cases which were not capital such as assaults the right of appeal indeed actually merged in an action of tort for damages, but this did not take place in the case of murder, or more serious offences, such as mayhem or robbery.

The accounts given in the older authorities of appeals for murder leave no doubt whatever that they took their origin in the primitive custom of vengeance of blood. The right of exacting vengeance was a privilege as well as a duty, and conferred by English, in the same way as by primitive Hebrew Law, upon the nearest relative of the deceased. "If there be anyone who would seek vengeance of the death by appeal of felony, let the male, of whatsoever age he be, be received before the female, and the next of blood before one more remote" (*a*).

The execution of the sentence too was left to the relatives of the murdered man. Blackstone tells us that it was an ancient usage which lasted until the reign of Henry IV, for the relatives of the slain to drag the appellee to the place of execution. This was manifestly a survival of primitive usage when the avenger of blood slew the murderer without any formal trial whatsoever.

Originally the right of an injured party to an appeal had priority to the King's right of proceeding by indictment. The appellant, however, was obliged to sue within a year and a day. Thus the laws of Edward I. provide that:—"As to larcenies and robberies committed in time of peace, where the offenders were not freshly pursued, the owners of the things shall have their suit by appeal of felony within the year and day, as in other felonies; but after that time their right of appeal shall cease, and the suit shall be ours. It is equally so

(*a*) Britton, liv. I., chap. ii., s. 7. See also Bracton, *De Legibus Angliae*, vol. ii., p. 309.

within the year and day, if no other suit is commenced, and so in all manner of felonies. And if the demandants bring their suit in form of trespass, they shall be heard, if they have not before commenced their suit in form of felony, in which case they cannot, by withdrawing from their suit, deprive us of ours. But where they have sued in form of trespass, although our peace may have been broken, we will not prosecute" (Britton, bk. I., ch. xxv., s. 6).

Previous to the statute 3 Hen. VII. cap. i. no person was ever put on his trial by indictment at the suit of the King until the year and the day had expired. And this appears to have been the origin of the curious rule in our law that a man cannot be indicted for murder, unless the death of the victim has taken place within a year and a day of the date of his receiving the fatal injury. The statute which enacted that indictments at the suit of the King might immediately be proceeded upon, and, before appeal brought, fully recognizes, however, the right which the heir-at-law had at Common Law to bring an appeal for the death of his ancestor, and prevent the acquittal of the appellee from being an effectual bar to the suit, though apparently a decision of the appeal in favour of the appellee was a bar to a subsequent indictment. The appellee was deprived of his right of trial by battle if there existed a violent presumption of his guilt, as if in an appeal of death, a man were taken with a bloody knife in his hand. (Staunford, *Pleas of the Crown*, bk. iii. c. 13. p. 178). In Bracton's time these presumptions led to immediate execution, but in the time of Staunford they were only held to oust the defendant of his wager of battle, and to compel him to put himself upon the country, as if he were accused by the King, or by a person, such as a woman, or infant under fourteen years of age, who in consequence of physical infirmity was unable to wage battle against the appellee.

In the case of an appeal the right of pardoning always rested with the appellant or plaintiff, not with the Crown. In fact it is distinctly laid down in several cases that the Crown had no right of pardon. In the fifth year of Elizabeth's reign in a case of *Stroughborough* v. *Biggon* (Moore, 571), an appeal was brought by a wife for the murder of her husband. The appellee was found guilty of manslaughter only. The question in the case was, whether the general pardon could pardon the burning in the hand, and, says the book, it was agreed that the Queen could not pardon it, and that the pardon could not operate thereon, because it was at the suit of the party. Whereupon the appellee compounded the prosecution for forty marks (see 3 Peere Williams, 453).

From the time of Elizabeth trial by appeal became practically obsolete. Two cases are mentioned as having been tried in the reign of Charles I., but after that reign there were none until at the end of the eighteenth century the practice was revived by some antiquarian lawyers, who were possibly stimulated thereto by the publication of Blackstone's Commentaries, the first edition of which was published in 1765. At all events we find that in the year 1770, an appeal was brought by one Anne Bigby against Matthew Kennedy and Patrick Kennedy for the murder of her husband. The case is fully reported in 5th *Burrowes*, at p. 2643.

"The following case of Bigby against the two Kennedyes," says the reporter, "is of so peculiar a nature, and upon a subject which occurs so very seldom, that I have been intentionally very minute and circumstantial in describing the method and form of proceeding in it; as I conceive that it may not only be an amusement to the curiosity of some readers, but may also be useful as a precedent, and save the trouble of searching into rule-books and records, whenever a future appeal shall happen to be brought. . . . As it is only a vindictive action, the proceedings are on the civil side of the court, and not the criminal, though the defendants are pursued not only criminally, but even capitally."

The case resulted in the escape of the defendants upon a technical point, and there was no further attempt to revive the practice until the year 1818, when the last instance of this antiquated procedure was tried in our courts. One Abraham Thornton had been tried on indictment for the rape and murder of a girl named Ashford. Though a strong case was made against him he was acquitted, owing to a flaw in the indictment, but as this was no bar to an appeal an attempt was made to bring him to justice by means of this form of action. The case is fully reported in 1 *Barnwall & Alderson's Reports* at page 405. The eldest brother and heir-at-law of the murdered girl was plaintiff or appellant in the suit. The following is a short sketch of the proceedings :—

The appellee (Thornton) having been brought into court and placed at the bar, claimed by his plea the right of trial by battle. He pleaded as follows. "Not guilty; and I am ready to defend the same by my body." And thereupon taking his glove off, he threw it upon the floor of the court. The appellant (Ashford) then put in a plea in reply stating strong circumstances of suspicion against the appellee with a view to depriving him of this right. This plea set out all the facts of the case, which appear upon the statement to have been almost conclusive of guilt. It concluded as follows :—

"And this, he, the said W. A. is ready to verify when, where, and in such manner as the Court here shall direct and award; wherefore he prays judgment, and that the said A. T. may not be admitted to wage battle in this appeal against him, the said W. A." The Court overruled this plea, and decided that the appellee was entitled to his wager of battle and that he could not be ousted of this right unless there existed such great and violent presumptions of guilt as would admit of no denial or proof to the contrary. "The general law of the land," said Lord Ellenborough, C. J., "is in favour of the wager of battel, and it is our duty to pronounce the law as it is, and not as we may wish it to be. Whatever prejudices therefore may justly exist against this mode of trial, still as it is the law of the land, the Court must pronounce judgment for it" (1 B. & Ald., p. 460).

"This mode of proceeding, by appeal," says Mr. Justice Bayley, "is unusual in our law, being brought, not for the benefit of the public, but for that of the party, and being a private suit, wholly under his control. It ought therefore to be watched very narrowly by the Court, for it may take place after trial and acquittal on an indictment at the suit of the King; and the execution under it is entirely at the option of the party suing, whose sole object it may be to obtain a pecuniary satisfaction. One inconvenience attending this mode of proceeding is, that the party who institutes it must be willing, if required, to stake his life in support of his accusation. For the battel is the right of the appellee at his election, unless he be excluded from it by some violent presumption of guilt existing against him" (1 B. & Ald., p. 457).

The "inconvenience attending this mode of proceeding" was fully illustrated in this the last instance of it, for the appellant declined the issue of battle. Whereupon the Court gave judgment that the appellee should go without day, and a man who in all probability had been guilty of a foul murder escaped scot-free. In the following year the procedure by way of appeal was wholly abolished by Act of Parliament (59 Geo. III. cap. 46).

Nothing illustrates so forcibly the strong conservative instinct of our law as the theoretical continuance, until the present century, of this system, with its barbarous accompaniments of trial by battle and pecuniary compositions for crime. It is astonishing how little alteration there was in English Law between the times of Bracton and Blackstone; less probably than there has been during the last hundred years, and this is true alike of Civil and Criminal Law.

True Criminal Law arose in England, as we have seen, in proceedings by the Sovereign to avenge personal wrongs to himself. By the fiction of a violation of his peace, whenever a crime was committed, the Crown was enabled to prosecute every offender, and in time it became the usual rule to do so, whether there was any real breach of the peace or not. But just as the procedure by way of appeal retained to the last the main features which originally distinguished it, so our modern Criminal Law retains in many respects, even to the present day, traces of its historical origin. The test, for instance, whether a libel is a criminal offence is still whether it tends to provoke a breach of the peace (*a*). If it does not, it only gives rise to a civil action for damages; but if it does, even though it is not communicated to any third person, but is contained in a letter addressed to the person defamed, it is a matter for indictment, the theory of the law being that it tends in that case to provoke a breach of the peace as much as if it were published (*b*). For the same reason, the truth of the libel is no defence to an indictment for publishing it, although it is an answer to an action for damages. "The greater the truth, the greater the libel" is the rule in criminal matters; and with good reason, for a defamatory statement certainly tends all the more for its truth to provoke hostility!

There are many other rules of Criminal Law which seem to us so natural that we can scarcely conceive them otherwise, but which owe their origin, as a matter of fact, to the accidental circumstance that the Crown prosecutes in all criminal cases. For instance, the general rule of English Law is that there is no prescription in criminal matters—no limit of time within which offences whether heinous or trifling must be prosecuted (*c*). This rule seems to us now so natural, that we are almost inclined to treat with ridicule any proposal to introduce a period of prescription into the Criminal Law; yet when we come to think of it, there does appear to be some unreasonableness in allowing a man to be prosecuted for stealing an article, when the article itself could not be recovered from him in a civil action. Most writers upon jurisprudence advocate a rule of prescription, at least as regards lesser offences (*d*). And in

(*a*) See *Reg.* v. *Adams*, 22 Q. B. D. 66.

(*b*) See 22 Q. B. D. at p. 68.

(*c*) Curiously enough there is a statutory exception to this rule in the case of treason. Prosecutions for treason must be commenced within three years from the commission of the offence, unless the treason consists of a designed assassination of the Sovereign (7 & 8 Wm. III. c. 3).

(*d*) See for instance Bentham, *Principles of Penal Code*, chap. iii., and Bertauld, *Cours de Code Pénal*, Leçon 25.

nearly every system of Criminal Law, except our own, the principle of prescription is adopted. According to the Roman Law, no crime could be prosecuted more than twenty years after its committal, and there were shorter periods of prescription in certain cases. According to the French Penal Code, the period is fixed at ten years for *crimes*, three years for *délits*, and one year for *contraventions* (Arts. 637, 638, and 640).

The absence of a rule of prescription in our Criminal Law is due altogether to a rigorous application of the maxim, "*nullum tempus occurrit regi.*" No time bars the King in seeking for a remedy against his subjects. The moral aspect of the question had apparently nothing to do with the matter, for we find that in the case of appeals there was a strict limit of a year and a day, within which the suit should be instituted.

Again, the right of pardon as a prerogative of the Crown took its origin historically in the fact that the King was supposed to be injured by a crime, and could therefore waive his remedy. There was no right of pardon vested in the Crown in the case of an appeal. "On an indictment which is at the suit of the King," says Blackstone (*a*), "the King may pardon and remit the execution; on an appeal which is at the suit of a private subject, to make an atonement for the private wrong, the King can no more pardon it than he can remit the damages recovered on an action of battery." The right of pardoning in the case of an appeal rested with the prosecutor not with the King. "As the King by his pardon may frustrate an indictment, so the appellant by his release may discharge an appeal" (*b*).

The curious offence of compounding a felony in our Law appears also to have originated in the system of Royal prosecutions. If a man forbears to prosecute a thief, upon being restored his own goods again he is in the eye of the law guilty of a criminal offence, punishable by fine and imprisonment, though few would consider him guilty of any moral delinquency. It is no offence to compound a misdemeanour; and such

(*a*) *Commentaries*, iv. 316. (*b*) *Ibid.*

a course is frequently actually encouraged by the Judge before whom the case is being tried. But misdemeanours are of comparatively recent origin in our Criminal Law : felonies were the crimes first recognized, and being offences against the King personally, to compound a felony was to prevent the King obtaining the redress to which he was entitled for the breach of his peace. Every loyal subject was bound to assist him in obtaining such redress. "To observe the commission of a felony without using any endeavours to apprehend the offender is a misprision" (1 Hale, P. C. 431), which was a wrong to the King, just in the same manner as misprision of treason or concealment of treasure-trove.

The doctrine of English Criminal Law, as regards the consent of the injured person to the act charged, probably arises in the same way. It is no defence to a prosecution for murder that the deceased agreed to take the risk of, or even consented to, his own death. Thus, if two men fight a duel, and one kill the other, he is guilty of murder; and it has been said that if two persons agree to assist each other in committing suicide, and one survives, he is guilty of murder (*R.* v. *Dyson*, R. & R. 523). The breach of the King's peace, not the wrong done to another person, is the gist of the crime. So, also, suicide was considered in the old law to be felony, and involved forfeiture of goods (Hawkins, P. C., chap. 27). Even in the case of an assault, if the act amounts to a breach of the peace, the consent of the person assaulted is no defence to the indictment.

"Whatever may be the effect of a consent in a suit between party and party, it is not in the power of any man to give an effectual consent to that which amounts to, or has a direct tendency to create, a breach of the peace, so as to bar a criminal prosecution. In other words, though a man may by his consent debar himself from his right to maintain a civil action, he cannot thereby defeat proceedings instituted by the Crown in the interests of the public for the maintenance of good order" (*per* Hawkins, J., *The Queen* v. *Coney*, 8 Q. B. D., at p. 553).

It would be easy to multiply instances showing the effect which the history of our Criminal Law has had upon its existing doctrines. It is impossible to understand this, or indeed any branch of law, without some knowledge of its history and origin.

INDEX.

THE END.

Printed by PONSONBY AND WELDRICK, *Dublin*.